Civil War Generals of the Union

Other Books in the History Makers Series:

Civil War Generals of the Union

By Diane Yancey

Lucent Books
P.O. Box 289011, San Diego, CA 92198-9011

Library of Congress Cataloging-in-Publication Data

Yancey, Diane.
    Civil War generals of the Union / by Diane Yancey.
        p.   cm. — (History makers)
    Includes bibliographical references and index.
    Summary: Focuses on the military careers of influential generals of the
Union Army during the Civil War.
    ISBN 1-56006-022-0 (lib. bdg.   :   alk. paper)
    1. Generals—United States—Biography—Juvenile literature.
2. United States. Army—Biography—Juvenile literature.   3. United
States—History—Civil War, 1861–1865—Biography—Juvenile literature.
[1. Generals. 2. United States. Army. 3. United States—History—
Civil War, 1861–1865—Biography.]   I. Title.   II. Series.
E467.D53   1999
973.7'3'0922—dc21   98-19560
[B]   CIP
                                                                 AC

CONTENTS

FOREWORD

The literary form most often referred to as "multiple biography" was perfected in the first century A.D. by Plutarch, a perceptive and talented moralist and historian who hailed from the small town of Chaeronea in central Greece. His most famous work, *Parallel Lives*, consists of a long series of biographies of noteworthy ancient Greek and Roman statesmen and military leaders. Frequently, Plutarch compares a famous Greek to a famous Roman, pointing out similarities in personality and achievements. These expertly constructed and very readable tracts provided later historians and others, including playwrights like Shakespeare, with priceless information about prominent ancient personages and also inspired new generations of writers to tackle the multiple biography genre.

The Lucent History Makers series proudly carries on the venerable tradition handed down from Plutarch. Each volume in the series consists of a set of six to eight biographies of important and influential historical figures who were linked together by a common factor. In *Rulers of Ancient Rome*, for example, all the figures were generals, consuls, or emperors of either the Roman Republic or Empire; while the subjects of *Fighters Against American Slavery*, though they lived in different places and times, all shared the same goal, namely the eradication of human servitude. Mindful that politicians and military leaders are not (and never have been) the only people who shape the course of history, the editors of the series have also included representatives from a wide range of endeavors, including scientists, artists, writers, philosophers, religious leaders, and sports figures.

Each book is intended to give a range of figures—some well known, others less known; some who made a great impact on history, others who made only a small impact. For instance, by making Columbus's initial voyage possible, Spain's Queen Isabella I, featured in *Women Leaders of Nations*, helped to open up the New World to exploration and exploitation by the European powers. Unarguably, therefore, she made a major contribution to a series of events that had momentous consequences for the entire world. By contrast, Catherine II, the eighteenth-century Russian queen, and Golda Meir, the modern Israeli prime minister, did not play roles of global impact; however, their policies and actions significantly influenced the historical development of both their own countries and their regional neighbors. Regardless of their relative importance in the greater historical scheme, all of the figures chronicled in the History Makers series made contributions to posterity; and their public achievements, as well as what is known about their private lives, are presented and evaluated in light of the most recent scholarship.

In addition, each volume in the series is documented and substantiated by a wide array of primary and secondary source quotations. The primary source quotes enliven the text by presenting eyewitness views of the times and culture in which each history maker lived; while the secondary source quotes, taken from the works of respected modern scholars, offer expert elaboration and/or critical commentary. Each quote is footnoted, demonstrating to the reader exactly where biographers find their information. The footnotes also provide the reader with the means of conducting additional research. Finally, to further guide and illuminate readers, each volume in the series features photographs, a chronology, two bibliographies, and a comprehensive index.

The History Makers series provides both students engaged in research and more casual readers with informative, enlightening, and entertaining overviews of individuals from a variety of circumstances, professions, and backgrounds. No doubt all of them, whether loved or hated, benevolent or cruel, constructive or destructive, will remain endlessly fascinating to each new generation seeking to identify the forces that shaped their world.

An Untested Company

Hundreds of generals fought for the Union in the Civil War. Most were relatively young, the average around thirty-eight years old. Many were professional men—lawyers, doctors, politicians. A few were teachers, farmers, and frontiersmen. All had one thing in common: a desire to fight for the Union even though most had no idea of the sacrifice that fight would entail. Historian Bruce Catton writes, "The country [went] to war gaily, it was all abubble . . . with flags and oratory and bands and training camps where life beat clerking all hollow [was better than ordinary work]; but ahead there was unutterable grimness." [1]

Trial and Error

Despite the enthusiasm, the Union war effort was hampered from the beginning by a lack of experienced commanders. Fewer than half of those who led had been regular army officers or had been educated at a military school. A great number were inexperienced civilians, having achieved their rank through political connections. Only two—Winfield Scott and John E. Wool—had had experience commanding large numbers of troops in battle, and both these men were well over seventy years old. Scott, commanding general of the army, was too fat to mount his horse. Wool was forgetful and needed help putting his hat on straight.

When faced with practicalities on the battlefield, Union generals often learned by trial and error, sometimes with disastrous results. Historian Shelby Foote notes, "The generals didn't know their jobs, the soldiers didn't know their jobs; it was just pure determination to stand and fight and not retreat, and the bloodiness of it was just astounding to everyone." [2]

The most effective leaders proved to be those with cool heads, a great deal of common sense, and the ability to learn from their mistakes. A certain cold-bloodedness was necessary as well, since almost all had to take responsibility for sending thousands of men to their deaths. Some of the most promising commanders found that their willingness to fight decreased as that responsibility grew. Others had the nerve and the temperament to stifle their doubts and regrets and focus on the ultimate goal—restoring the Union and bringing the killing to an end.

Key Players

Many Union commanders deserve notice for their contributions, their characters, or their moments of glory during the war. George Armstrong Custer, later famous for his role in the tragedy at the Little Bighorn, became a general at the age of twenty-three and was one of Sheridan's most reckless and intrepid cavalrymen. Quiet, scholarly Joshua Lawrence Chamberlain taught himself military tactics while in camp, then used an almost forgotten textbook maneuver to help save the Union Army at Gettysburg. Solid George H. Thomas was dubbed "the Rock of Chickamauga" after firmly holding his line in the face of defeat at the Battle of Chickamauga in 1863.

The handful of generals in this book were selected from among many for several reasons. First, most were key players in the war:

Union soldiers pose for a photograph with one of their mighty cannons. Despite the inexperience of its soldiers and generals, the Union emerged as the war's victor.

George McClellan, the charismatic hero; William Tecumseh Sherman, one of the most talented strategists of all time; Philip Sheridan, crack cavalryman; and Ulysses S. Grant, who gave the Union a "grand offensive" and finally brought the war to an end.

Other generals are less well known but colorful representatives of men who played similar roles in the war. Amiable, well-intentioned Ambrose Burnside was one of the men whom Lincoln hoped might lead the Army of the Potomac to victory. Like his colleagues George Meade, Joseph Hooker, and John Pope, however, Burnside lacked the ability to successfully handle the job.

Benjamin Butler, the most hated general of the war, represents commanders who enforced military law in occupied Southern towns while fighting was going on elsewhere. Butler, a ruthless overseer and shrewd politician, left New Orleans cleaner, healthier, and more orderly than it had been for years prior to Union occupation.

Men of War

The Union generals served their country at a time when the fate of the United States hung in the balance. Some of these men died before the final victory. A few lived to see World War One. For the

Highest Rank

The United States Army is the oldest branch of the nation's military, dating back to June 1775, when the Continental Congress created the Continental Army to fight in the Revolutionary War. George Washington was elected commander in chief of the army at about that time, and later was commissioned lieutenant general. In the United States and many other countries, the highest officers of the army, air force, and marine corps bear the rank of general.

Congress created the rank of General of the Army in 1866 and awarded it to Ulysses S. Grant, also promoting him from lieutenant general to full general. In their lifetimes, Civil War heroes William T. Sherman and Philip H. Sheridan also served as General of the Army.

Today, the U.S. Army has five orders of general, the highest being General of the Army. An officer holding this rank wears the insignia of five stars. The next level is "general," also known as full general, and carries with it four stars. "Lieutenant general" follows with three stars, "major general" with two, and "brigadier general" with one. Five heroes of World War Two became five-star generals: Henry H. Arnold, Omar N. Bradley, Dwight D. Eisenhower, Douglas MacArthur, and George C. Marshall.

Ulysses S. Grant (seated in armchair) and his generals—including George Meade (front row, second from right), William Sherman (front row, center), and Philip Sheridan (front row, far left)—gather in Washington, D.C., in 1866.

sake of patriotism and duty, however, all took part in the bloody fight that soon became epic in its proportions. Bruce Catton writes, "Here was the greatest and most moving chapter in American history, a blending of meanness and greatness, an ending and a beginning. It came out of what men were, but it did not go as men had planned. The Almighty had his own purposes."[3]

CHAPTER 1

A Personal War

The Civil War was a personal war, fought in American front yards, cornfields, and peach orchards across the country. American homes were headquarters for troops on both sides. American churches and schools were used to house the wounded and dying.

Americans from all walks of life viewed the war from their own personal perspectives. To the abolitionist, it was a struggle over human rights; to Abraham Lincoln, a battle to save the Union. Men like Benjamin Butler viewed it as a chance to get rich. Others—particularly the 3 million men who left their homes for the battlefields—saw it simply as the "greatest adventure of their lives."[4]

Sectionalism and States' Rights

The adventure began on April 12, 1861, when Confederate troops fired on Fort Sumter, a U.S. Army post set in the harbor of Charleston, South Carolina. The roots of the war lay far in the past, however.

Sectionalism, narrow-minded devotion to the interests of one section of the country, was one of the leading causes of the war. This bias originated in colonial times when early settlers discovered that the warm climate and rich soil of the South was ideal for growing crops such as tobacco, cotton, and sugar beets. Such crops could not be grown in the colder, rockier northern states, whose economies began to rely on industry and trade more than agriculture.

Differences between North and South grew even greater over time as Southerners brought in slaves and developed a slow-paced, agrarian society with time set aside for cultural pursuits and gracious living. People in the North, on the other hand, became modern, fast-paced, and urban as industry grew. Northerners looked to the future, and valued hard work, education, and independence. Unlike Southerners who placed emphasis on states' rights, most Northerners believed that federal laws took precedence over those of individual states, and that communities had the right to decide whether policies were moral or immoral. One such policy was the institution of slavery.

A Civil War–era photograph shows the battered interior of Fort Sumter, where the Confederate army launched the first salvos of war.

The Sleeping Serpent

Slavery had been a source of controversy in the United States since colonial times. "There was never a moment in our history when slavery was not a sleeping serpent," wrote essayist and poet John Jay Chapman.[5] But since most Americans perceived it as a "necessary evil," the Founding Fathers had not included in the Constitution a clause banning the practice.

By the 1800s, slavery had become widespread in the South, and the gap between Northern and Southern attitudes was deep and wide. It grew wider as the movement to abolish slavery—to eliminate it altogether—gained strength in the North. "I am in earnest. I will not equivocate. I will not excuse. I will not retreat a single inch, and I will be heard," vowed publisher William Lloyd Garrison in a call for abolition in 1831.[6]

At the same time, Southerners grew increasingly certain that their economy would collapse without slaves. Many Southerners also convinced themselves that slavery was morally justifiable since, in their opinion, Negroes were lazy, stupid, and in need of constant care and supervision.

"A House Divided"

The controversy over slavery and states' rights was not confined to discussions around dinner tables and on street corners. In the

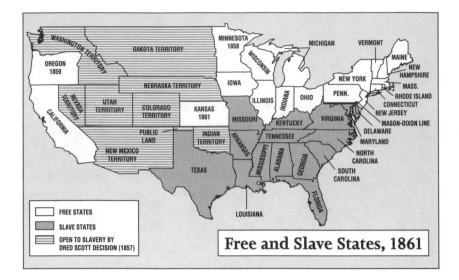

Free and Slave States, 1861

FREE STATES
SLAVE STATES
OPEN TO SLAVERY BY
DRED SCOTT DECISION (1857)

1850s, an ongoing debate between Northern and Southern law-makers sometimes broke out into actual violence on the floor of the House and Senate. Such was the case in May 1856, when South Carolina congressman Preston Brooks severely caned Senator Charles Sumner of Massachusetts after Sumner gave a speech denouncing South Carolina senator Andrew Butler's devotion to "the harlot slavery." [7] Brooks was Butler's nephew.

In the election of 1860, the newly formed Republican Party nominated as their candidate for president Abraham Lincoln, a moderate who opposed the spread of slavery. When Lincoln won the election, Southerners believed he threatened their way of life. In December 1861, South Carolina made the decision to secede (withdraw) from the Union, now viewed as an oppressor poised to violate the state's rights.

In the next few months, ten other Southern states seceded: Mississippi, Florida, Alabama, Georgia, Louisiana, Texas, Virginia, Tennessee, Arkansas, and North Carolina. On February 1, 1861, Jefferson Davis was sworn in as president of the newly formed Provisional Confederate States of America, with Richmond, Virginia, designated as its capital. The Confederacy's objectives included the preservation of slavery and an emphasis on states' rights. Many Southerners believed so strongly in this last principle that they weakened the Confederate government by their refusal to relinquish power and cooperate with other states and leaders during the war.

The initial objective of the North, as expressed by Abraham Lincoln, was the preservation of the Union in its entirety. "A house divided against itself cannot stand," he said before the war began. "I do not expect the house to fall, but I do expect it will cease to be divided. It will become all one thing or all the other." [8] As time passed, the issue of slavery also grew in importance until it all but eclipsed the primary objective of preserving the Union. "The American people and the government of Washington may refuse to recognize it for a time, but the inexorable logic of events will force it upon them in the end—that the war now being waged in this land is a war for and against slavery," declared Frederick Douglass, a former slave who became a spokesman for Negro rights. [9]

Abraham Lincoln supported Douglass's contention by issuing the Emancipation Proclamation on January 1, 1863. This order freed only slaves in Confederate states; it did not apply to slaves in slave states that remained in the Union. In 1865, however, Congress passed the Thirteenth Amendment to the Constitution, which abolished slavery nationwide.

Southern politician Jefferson Davis presided over the newly formed Confederate States of America.

Unprepared for War

Initially the war was met with plenty of enthusiasm and commitment on both sides. "There are but two parties now, traitors and patriots, and I want hereafter to be ranked with the latter," stated Ulysses S. Grant as he joined a Union regiment in Illinois. [10] Most people believed that the war would last only a few months, and young men hurried to join before it could end. Those unable to enlist immediately cursed their missed opportunity to whip the enemy. Men like William Tecumseh Sherman, who foresaw the prolonged agony of the conflict, were branded "crazy" by newspaper reporters.

The causes of the war were longstanding, however, not likely to be quickly settled. The South had fewer numbers—only 9 million inhabitants (4 million of those were slaves), while the Northern population stood at about 21 million at the beginning of the war—but Southerners viewed the conflict as an invasion of their homeland. Thus they were motivated to fight fiercely in an effort

President Abraham Lincoln meets with his advisers during the official signing of the Emancipation Proclamation on January 1, 1863.

to defend their homes, a factor that tended to even the odds. Southern chances also were improved by the availability of talented leaders such as Thomas "Stonewall" Jackson, Pierre G. T. Beauregard, J. E. B. Stuart, and Robert E. Lee, who had been trained at the U.S. Military Academy at West Point, New York. Despite their talents, however, neither they nor Northern generals initially understood the strategy that would prove necessary to win a large-scale conflict. After several fierce battles, both sides conceded that it would take years, not months, to bring the war to a conclusion.

In the first two years of the war, the South's fighting spirit seemed likely to carry the day. Battles to capture towns and disrupt transportation became Confederate victories. It seemed almost unbelievable to Northerners that upstart Southern armies could repeatedly beat back and humiliate the United States Army. In the ultimate embarrassment, Jeb Stuart's Confederate cavalrymen departed unscathed after making a three-day, one-hundred-fifty-mile circuit of the Army of the Potomac, burning Federal (Union) camps, capturing horses and mules, and cutting telegraph wires.

Northerners finally realized, however, that their army's weakness lay in its generals rather than its fighting men. A scarcity of leaders willing to vigorously pursue the enemy, send men to certain death on the battlefield, and bring the South to its knees contributed to lackluster Union results in the early years. "No general yet found can face the arithmetic, but the end of the war will be at hand when he shall be discovered," Abraham Lincoln predicted.[11]

Bloody Battlefields

While President Lincoln and the War Department searched in vain for someone who could lead Union armies to victory, the fighting continued. Many battles took place in Virginia, perilously close to the nation's capital, Washington, D.C. Others were fought in "the West," states lying west of the Appalachian Mountains but east of

Put It Through!

The early years of the Civil War were an exasperating time for Northerners, particularly Abraham Lincoln, who could not find "fighting" generals to lead his armies. Lincoln's frustration is described by T. Harry Williams in Lincoln and His Generals.

"Much of Lincoln's so-called interfering with the conduct of the war occurred in the first years of the conflict, when he believed, with some reason, that he was more capable of managing operations than were most of the generals. When the war started, he was inclined to defer to the judgments of trained soldiers. He soon came to doubt and even scorn the capabilities of the military mind. He asked of the generals decision, action, fighting, victory. They replied with indecision, inaction, delay, excuses. He became oppressed by the spectacle, so familiar in war, of generals who were superb in preparing for battle but who shrank from seeking its awful decision. 'Tell him,' he wrote in preparing instructions for one general, 'to put it through—not to be writing or telegraphing back here, but put it through.' He wanted victories, but he got more letters than victories, letters from generals who wrote back that they could not put it through unless Lincoln provided them with more men and more guns . . . and still more."

During the early years of the Civil War, Abraham Lincoln searched for a general who was skilled at both diplomacy and the art of warfare.

the Mississippi River. The heart of the Confederacy lay in the east, but the Mississippi River was a vital means of transportation, and many bloody encounters—the most significant at Vicksburg and New Orleans—took place as both sides tried to control it. The greatest battle ever fought in the Western Hemisphere, the Battle of Gettysburg, took place in southern Pennsylvania in July 1863. The contest lasted for three days, involved 150,000 men, and resulted in over 40,000 casualties. Gettysburg marked the turning point in the war, since Robert E. Lee lost so many men that he was not able to launch another major offensive.

Many of the battles of the Civil War were bloodier than any fought before. At the Battle of Shiloh (Pittsburg Landing, Tennessee), more Americans were killed than had died in all other wars fought on American soil up to that time. In the Battle of Stones River (Murfreesboro, Tennessee), each side lost about a third of its men. And in the Battle of Cold Harbor (Virginia), the North lost seven thousand men in twenty minutes. Historian Bruce Catton notes, "The Army of the Potomac was half destroyed . . . but it was carrying out its appointed assignment. Somewhere far ahead there would be victory, even if most of the men who had made it possible would not be around to see it." [12]

A young Confederate soldier lies dead after the bloody Battle of Gettysburg. The three-day battle claimed forty thousand casualties.

Unprepared for War

Convinced that the South would never secede from the Union, the North was almost totally unprepared for war in 1861. Chief among its deficiencies was a lack of geographical information needed to do battle, as historian T. Harry Williams points out in Lincoln and His Generals.

"One of the most ironic examples of American military unreadiness was the spectacle of Northern—and Southern—generals fighting in their own country and not knowing where they were going or how to get there. Before the war the government had collected no topographical information about neighboring counties or even the United States, except for the West. No accurate military maps existed. General Henry W. Halleck was running a campaign in the western theater in 1862 with maps he got from a book store. . . . [One] civil engineer drew a map for a general going into western Virginia, but the best he could promise was that it would not *mislead* the expedition. General George B. McClellan had elaborate maps prepared for his Virginia campaign of 1862 and found to his dismay when he arrived on the scene that they were unreliable; 'the roads are wrong . . . ,' he wailed. Not until 1863 did the Army of the Potomac have an accurate map of northern Virginia, its theater of operations."

"One Hand Behind Its Back"

The North lost more men in the war than the South—360,000 compared to 260,000—but from the beginning the Confederacy was at a disadvantage, with fewer reserves of men and materials. Southern troop losses became irreplaceable when almost every man and boy had been called to the field. Limited Southern resources were also used up, and the Union's naval blockade prevented imports. While inflation and the scarcity of necessities such as food, clothes, and shoes hampered the Confederate war effort, Northern mills and factories continued to produce an abundance of guns, food, and military supplies, and significant numbers of men never were called to serve their country. Historian Shelby Foote observes:

> I think that the North fought [the Civil War] with one hand behind its back. At the same time the war was going on . . . all these marvelous inventions were going on. In the Spring of '64 the Harvard/Yale boat races were going on and not a man in either crew ever volunteered for the army or the

navy. They didn't need them. I think that if [there] had been more Southern successes . . . the North simply would have brought that other arm out from behind its back.[13]

Ending and Beginning

The appointment of Ulysses Grant as general in chief of all Union armies in March 1864 marked the beginning of the end of the Civil War. Grant did not follow the pattern of other Northern generals who sometimes hesitated to attack the enemy. He realized that the war would be won only when the Confederacy was too weak to continue fighting, and he tenaciously hammered Southern forces until he achieved the ultimate victory.

General Ulysses S. Grant ably commanded the Union army to victory in the Civil War.

That victory was acknowledged on April 9, 1865, when Lee surrendered his Army of Northern Virginia in the village of Appomattox Court House, Virginia. With the surrender, the character of the country changed. Henceforth the phrases "one nation, indivisible," and "all men are created equal" took on new meaning in the United States.

Before that could happen, however, all Americans had to pass through the fiery trial that would pit brother against brother, and turn friends into enemies. A train of Union generals marched courageously but ineffectively in and out of the high command before Grant arrived. The first and most promising, George McClellan, described them all when he said, "Their honesty and sincerity were proved by the sacrifices they made . . . and by the readiness with which so many brave men laid down their lives on the field of battle." [14]

CHAPTER 2

Young Napoleon

On July 27, 1861, just three months after the first shots of the Civil War were fired, Major General George B. McClellan stepped off the train in Washington, D.C. The thirty-four-year-old confidently surveyed the bustling city and its citizens, who had recently been dismayed by the Union army's defeat at Bull Run (Manassas). McClellan had been summoned to the city by President Abraham Lincoln and General in Chief Winfield Scott in hopes that he would be able to lead the Union to victory against rebellious Southerners who had seceded earlier that year. There was no doubt in McClellan's mind that he was the man for the job.

A Natural Leader

Although much of George Brinton McClellan's career is well documented, little is recorded of his early life. He was born on December 3, 1826, and his sister Fredericka affectionately described him as "the brightest, merriest, most unselfish of boys . . . [fond] of fun and frolic, and always the 'soul of honor.' " [15] His father was a physician; his mother came from a well-to-do Philadelphia family. At the

Born in 1826, George B. McClellan was only thirty-four years old when he assumed command of the Army of the Potomac.

age of six he began attending a private school run by Harvard graduate Sears Cook Walker; then he was privately tutored until 1838, when he enrolled in a preparatory academy affiliated with the University of Pennsylvania. "Before I went to West Point, I had received an excellent classical education, was well read in History for a boy, and was a good French scholar," he remembered.[16] While at the academy, McClellan was accused of an infraction he had not committed. The headmaster prepared to punish the boy, who later wrote, "My father had told me not to permit myself to be whipped, [so] I met him with a kick and went out of [was expelled from] school." [17] The dispute was settled in a few days, and McClellan returned to his studies with no further trouble.

A gifted student, McClellan entered the University of Pennsylvania at the age of thirteen, intending to study law. He soon changed his mind, however, and in 1842, at the age of fifteen, entered the U.S. Military Academy at West Point, New York, the top military school in the country. At West Point, the dark, ruggedly handsome young man went to the head of his class while learning the fundamentals of being a soldier—how to dress properly, how to march, how to use the musket and bayonet. He was only five foot eight inches tall, but his confidence, friendliness, and athletic ability kept him from being overlooked, and he was popular with other well-bred young men, many of whom would also become leaders in the coming war.

In the spring of 1846, McClellan graduated second in his class and was commissioned a second lieutenant in the Corps of Engineers, an elite group of highly accomplished graduates who were expected to perform such tasks as constructing military roads and bridges and designing fortifications and batteries (banks of heavy guns). "We were taught with every breath we drew at West Point . . . that the engineers were a species of gods," wrote John Tidball, a lower classman.[18] Hopeful that his new assignment would be a path to further study of military science, his real interest, McClellan headed south to be part of the war being waged between the United States and Mexico.

In the Mexican campaign, McClellan distinguished himself and came away with an appreciation for siege tactics, wherein an army encircles and blockades the enemy until he surrenders, rather than engaging in bloody head-on assaults. After coping with the ignorance and incompetence of politically appointed officers, he also developed a dislike for civilians who interfered in military affairs. These were qualities that would guide his thinking in the years 1861 to 1862, when he led the Army of the Potomac.

Union Man

In the years immediately following the Mexican War, McClellan returned to West Point as a member of the faculty. He filled his spare time by hunting, fishing, and reminiscing with friends. "What pleasure it is to get with some comrade of the war & talk ('gas' as we say) over old times," he wrote.[19] He also enjoyed studying history and the art of war. In 1855, a member of a military party, he traveled to Europe to observe and report on the war in the Crimea.

McClellan returned to the United States with a reputation as a military authority. He had seen war firsthand and had learned how to train, supply, and transport large numbers of men. His knowledge of European and Russian cavalry regulations was incorporated into a manual he wrote for the American cavalry, and in the words of one of his associates, he was "chock full of big war science." [20]

Before civil war broke out in the United States, however, McClellan had left the army and was pursuing a successful career as president of the Eastern Division of the Ohio and Mississippi Railroad. In 1860 he married charming Mary Ellen Marcy after a long courtship, and the young couple settled into a comfortable home in Cincinnati. Despite their busy social life, the two were very close, and for the rest of his life, McClellan wrote to his wife daily whenever they were separated. "Whatever the future may have in store for me you will be the chief actor in that play," he vowed.[21]

McClellan was no abolitionist, but he ardently believed in the Union, and thus, when Fort Sumter was shelled, he felt his duty lay in service to the North. "The Govt is in danger, our flag insulted & we must stand by it," he told one friend in 1861.[22] In high demand from several states, he accepted a command in Ohio, and with great energy and efficiency, began to organize and shape his men into an army. One observer wrote, "Personally he was a very charming man, and his manner of doing business impressed every one with the belief that he knew what he was about." [23]

Command

McClellan was soon known for his competence and for his popularity with both men and officers. On May 3, 1861, he was given command of the Department of the Ohio, overseeing all troops in Ohio, Indiana, and Illinois. On May 14, as a result of the efforts of Treasury secretary Salmon P. Chase, who hailed from Ohio, he was awarded the army's highest rank at the time, that of major general in the regular army. It was an important honor; only Winfield Scott outranked him.

McClellan definitively proved his capability as a military leader that summer, when he led a campaign into western Virginia to establish a Union foothold there. After a series of skirmishes and minor battles, he achieved a relatively easy victory and was rewarded with a flood of recognition and praise that made him an overnight national hero. The *New York Times* proclaimed, "We feel very proud of our wise and brave young Major-General," and the *New York Herald* dedicated a congratulatory column to "Gen. McClellan, the Napoleon of the Present War." [24] Soon others were comparing him to Napoleon Bonaparte, military genius of the eighteenth century. Historian T. Harry Williams notes in *McClellan, Sherman and Grant*, "The acclaim for [McClellan] was tremendous and out of proportion to his deeds. But successful

George McClellan and Mary Ellen Marcy were wed in 1860. The couple maintained an extremely close relationship even when McClellan was called away by the war.

Conquering Hero

With his charm and good looks, George McClellan won popularity with many Americans from the early days of the war when he led his men to victory in western Virginia. In a letter to his wife, published in McClellan's Own Story, *he details the events of June 20, 1861.*

"We got off at 11.30 yesterday morning, and had a continual ovation all along the road. At every station where we stopped crowds had assembled to see the 'young general': gray-headed old men and women, mothers holding up their children to take my hand, girls, boys, all sorts, cheering and crying, God bless you! I never went through such a scene in my life, and never expect to go through such another one. You would have been surprised at the excitement. At Chillicothe [Ohio] the ladies had prepared a dinner, and I had to be trotted through. They gave me about twenty beautiful bouquets and almost killed me with kindness. The trouble will be to fill their expectations, they seem to be so high. I could hear them say, 'He is our own general'; 'Look at him, how young he is'; 'He will thrash them'; 'He'll do,' etc. etc."

Northern generals were so rare at the moment . . . [that] the young soldier out in the mountains seemed a veritable hero, an emerging genius."[25]

General Scott and President Lincoln did not necessarily view McClellan as a second Napoleon, but they did believe that he was better suited to lead the Army of the Potomac than General Irvin McDowell, its first commander. Thus, Scott requested that the young general come to Washington, D.C., to assume the new duties of commanding an army of thirty thousand men. No American general had ever been asked to take on such a gigantic task before.

"Power of the Land"

In July 1861, McClellan was appointed head of the Division of the Potomac, made up of what had been McDowell's army and the troops assigned to defend the capital. In November of the same year, when Winfield Scott retired, the young general was also named general in chief, and given charge of all the armies of the Union, east and west. Rather than living with troops outside Washington, he set up his headquarters in a spacious private home on Pennsylvania Avenue and became a familiar sight as he rushed from one appointment to another throughout the city.

Soldiers perform drills at their New York camp in 1861. Under the command of general in chief George McClellan, the armies of the Union were disciplined and drilled until they were confident in their abilities.

Initially, the size of his new command, with its heavy burden of responsibility, did not seem to bother McClellan. Under his wife's influence he had become deeply religious, and he was convinced that God had chosen him to save the Union. In addition, the attention he received was flattering. He wrote to his wife, "I find myself in a new and strange position here: President, Cabinet, Gen. Scott and all deferring to me. By some strange operation of magic I seem to have become the power of the land." [26]

His first task was to energize the discouraged veterans of Bull Run and bring order to masses of green recruits who made up the Army of the Potomac. McClellan spent hours organizing the camps and getting to know his men. He demanded discipline and hard work from his officers. Since flamboyant military displays exactly suited his romantic nature, he staged grand reviews to build the morale of his troops and civilian audiences. In just a few weeks, the army was in better form than ever before. T. Harry Williams notes, "Whatever else [McClellan] failed to do in the war, he created that army, and gave it a belief in itself that nothing could destroy." [27]

"One Safe Rule of War"

McClellan's work was exceptional, but soon the enormity of the task he had undertaken dawned on him. Information supplied from deserters and informers told him that the Confederate army, which lay just a few miles to the south, was a legion vastly larger than his own. On August 8, 1861, he wrote to General Scott, "I am induced to believe that the enemy has at least 100,000 men in

His Own Worst Enemy

McClellan was his own worst enemy in the Civil War, plagued by doubts and misconceptions, especially when it came to his view of the opposing military force. At the time of this letter, written to his wife on August 16, 1861, and published in McClellan's Own Story, *his troops numbered about fifty-five thousand; his opponent, the Confederate general P. G. T. Beauregard, had fewer than forty-five thousand.*

"I am here in a terrible place: the enemy have from three to four times my force; the President, [and] the old general [Scott], cannot or will not see the true state of affairs. Most of my troops are demoralized by the defeat at Bull Run; some regiments even mutinous. I have probably stopped that; but you see my position is not pleasant. . . . I have, I believe, made the best possible disposition of the few men under my command; will quietly await events, and, if the enemy attacks, will try to make my movements as rapid and desperate as may be. If my men will only fight I think I can thrash him, notwithstanding the disparity of numbers. As it is, I trust to God to give success to our arms, though He is not wont to aid those who refuse to aid themselves. . . . I am weary of all this. I have no ambition in the present affairs; only wish to save my country, and find the incapables around me will not permit it. They sit on the verge of the precipice, and cannot realize what they see."

McClellan (center) and his generals pose for a somber photograph at their headquarters in 1861.

our front."[28] Although the information was false, McClellan became convinced that the enemy was a fearsome force, which could not be defeated without careful preparation and increased numbers of men and arms.

Added to McClellan's fear of the enemy was his growing dislike and distrust of Lincoln and Scott, whom he believed were too ignorant and foolish to understand the true danger that threatened. "Gen. Scott is the most dangerous antagonist I have. Our ideas are so widely different that it is impossible for us to work together much longer," he wrote to his wife on August 13.[29] Although he spoke more kindly of the president, in private McClellan nicknamed him "the Gorilla" and sometimes snubbed him. In one instance while Lincoln patiently waited at McClellan's home for a meeting with the absent general, McClellan returned and went to bed, not bothering to convey that news to his guest waiting in the parlor downstairs.

Despite such displays of arrogance, McClellan felt threatened on all sides and so followed his "one safe rule of war"—prepare for the worst.[30] That meant calling for more troops, carefully weighing risks, and gathering information and supplies. Weeks passed, and Lincoln begged him to act, but he replied that he was not fully prepared and again asked for more troops. In the meantime his wife and baby daughter joined him in Washington, and once again the couple was caught up in the social scene. Soon it was winter, a time for receptions and dinner parties. McClellan did not say it, but his intentions were clear. War could be waged better in the spring.

During the winter the Union army continued to drill in camp, delaying the onset of war until spring.

Lincoln did not share this view. In March 1862, the president grew so impatient that he relieved McClellan of the position of general in chief, hoping that fewer responsibilities would free McClellan for more fighting. Although he took the disappointment well, McClellan privately believed that the act was an enormous mistake on Lincoln's part. "The order proved to be one of the steps taken to tie my hands in order to secure the failure of the approaching campaign," he wrote in his memoirs.[31]

The Peninsular Campaign

Still commander of the Army of the Potomac, McClellan set out in the spring of 1862 on what became known as the Peninsular campaign. His goal—to take the Confederate capital of Richmond, Virginia, demoralize the South, and bring the war to an early end.

The campaign began as a monumental procession made up of over 121,000 men, 14,000 horses and mules, 1,100 wagons, 44 batteries of artillery, plus ambulances, tents, telegraph wires, pontoons for bridges, and tons of provisions. On May 5, the Union force saw its first skirmish with Confederates near Williamsburg, Virginia. McClellan, who was at his headquarters ten miles behind the lines when the fighting began, did not arrive until the Confederates were in retreat. Instead of pursuing them, he waited until morning, then ordered the slow trek up the Peninsula to continue.

At the end of the month, McClellan's army again faced Confederate attack near Fair Oaks, Virginia. This time the general was in bed with a severe attack of malaria, yet his surprised men put up a strong fight against General Joseph E. Johnston. The battle ended in a virtual standoff, but at its end, one significant factor had changed. Johnston had been seriously wounded, and Robert E. Lee had taken his command. Lee, who would lead the Army of Northern Virginia until the end of the war, proved more than a match for McClellan and the Army of the Potomac for months to come.

General Without an Army

Although the nation gave McClellan credit for Union successes at Williamsburg and Fair Oaks, his slowness and his failure to take the offensive displeased Lincoln, who desperately wanted to end the war quickly. McClellan proved that he could fight during the Battle of Seven Days in June 1862, but he fought defensively, unnerved by Lee's hard-hitting tactics and the alleged size of the enemy army. He wrote to E. M. Stanton, the secretary of war:

> I have not a man in reserve and shall be glad to cover my retreat and save the material and *personnel* of the Army.

Union soldiers defend the Federal battery at Fair Oaks, Virginia, during McClellan's Peninsular campaign of 1862.

> . . . I have lost this battle because my force was too small. I again repeat that I am not responsible for this, and I say it with the earnestness of a general who feels in his heart the loss of every brave man who has been needlessly sacrificed today.[32]

In August 1862, newly appointed general in chief, Henry W. Halleck, recalled McClellan and his army from the Peninsula. Major General John Pope, head of the Army of Virginia, was actively fighting Confederates in northern Virginia, and he needed all the reinforcements he could get. Soon, most of the Army of the Potomac were reallocated to Pope, while disgruntled McClellan became a general without an army. "It is dreadful to listen to this cannonading and not be able to take any part in it," he wrote to his wife, Ellen. "I feel too blue and disgusted to write any more now, so I will smoke a cigar and try to get into a better humor." [33]

Fortunately for McClellan, Pope's command of the Army of the Potomac was brief. The Union experienced a second defeat at Bull Run, and shortly thereafter Lincoln relieved Pope, and reluctantly replaced him with McClellan. In the president's opinion, McClellan was too slow and cautious, but he was a good organizer and he had the knack of encouraging defeated and demoralized troops.

McClellan himself seemed unaware of the president's hesitation. He wrote to his wife, "Again I have been called upon to save the country. The case is desperate, but with God's help I will try unselfishly to do my best, and, if he wills it, accomplish the salvation of the nation." [34]

Ready to Fight

Again commander of the Army of the Potomac, McClellan set about restoring confidence in the camps. His presence alone was a morale booster. Within five days, "Little Mac" as he was affectionately called, had given his troops a new desire to fight for their commander and their country. "McClellan's reappointment gives great satisfaction to the soldiers," wrote one officer. "Whether right or wrong they believe in him." [35] And Lincoln told his secretary John Hay, "He excels in making others ready to fight." [36]

McClellan did indeed appear ready to fight as he left Washington to meet Lee's army, which had invaded Maryland in September. On September 8, he wrote to Halleck, "As soon as I find out where to strike I will be after them [Lee's army] without an hour's delay." [37] But it was over a week later before the two armies met near the town of Sharpsburg, Maryland, on the banks of Antietam Creek.

The battle proved the bloodiest of the Civil War thus far. McClellan waited too long before attacking, allowing Confederate reinforcements to arrive. With typical caution, he also held some of his troops in reserve, weakening his offensive. His men fought valiantly, but by the end of the day, Lee's lines of defense were still unbroken, his army still able to fight. Confederate casualties were high, but Union dead and wounded numbered eleven thousand.

General McClellan, or "Little Mac" as his troops affectionately nicknamed him, proved to be an inspiring leader.

The Confederates, battered and vulnerable, expected McClellan to renew his attack the following morning. Morning arrived, however, and the order did not come. Soldiers on both sides speculated as to what the respite might mean. One Union soldier wrote in his diary, "Rumor no. 5. Little McC has given the Rebs 7 hours to make up their minds whether they will surrender." [38]

Surrender was far from Lee's mind. Familiar with McClellan's hesitancy, he took the opportunity to retreat back into Virginia.

McClellan did not stop him. The Union had pushed the enemy back and secured the safety of Washington. To him, that was a sufficient accomplishment. He wrote to his wife, "God has, in His mercy, a second time made me the instrument for saving the nation." [39]

Relieved of Command

It was the last victory for which McClellan could claim responsibility. In the days and weeks after the battle, the general remained in camp, demanding more reinforcements and insisting that his

President Lincoln confers with General McClellan in his camp at Antietam, site of the bloodiest battle of the Civil War.

men needed rest. Lincoln urged him to fight, even going so far as to issue a direct order to march the Army of the Potomac south toward Richmond. McClellan obeyed, but he willfully took a slow, circuitous route, averaging slightly more than three miles per day. Lee marched his men twice as far in half the time.

It was the final blow to Lincoln's patience. On November 5, he sent a special courier from Washington to McClellan's camp, removing him from command. As the president later explained, he had "tried long enough to bore with an auger too dull to take hold." [40]

McClellan took the order calmly, hiding the anger and hurt he must have felt. He spent several days helping his successor, Ambrose Burnside, with the changeover, said good-bye to his men, and listened to their farewell cheers. On November 11, he boarded a train bound for Washington, D.C. That day marked the end of his war career. McClellan was never given another duty assignment again.

A New Career

McClellan's military career had ended, but his popularity remained high. Wherever he went, he was met by bands, city officials, and cheering crowds. He took up residence in New York City, and the city's newspapers reported his every move as he attended grand balls, public dinners, the theater, and the opera. New York was a strong Democratic locale, and wealthy party leaders showed their admiration with the gift of a spacious home in one of Manhattan's most prestigious neighborhoods.

In the summer of 1864, McClellan, a longtime Democrat, accepted the Democratic nomination for president at the Chicago convention. He ran on a platform of compromise. The war, he stated, should be conducted "upon the highest principles known to Christian Civilization." [41] In addition, private property and unarmed persons should be protected from enemy forces, the abolition of slavery made voluntary, and slaveowners compensated for loss of property. If elected, he promised that he would try to negotiate with the South to bring the war to an early end.

To a nation weary of war, McClellan's promises were attractive, and Lincoln's chances of reelection appeared remote. On August 22, Henry J. Raymond, the Republican national chairman, wrote the president, "The tide is setting strongly against us." [42] Lincoln himself wrote a memorandum, which read:

> This morning, as for some days past, it seems exceedingly probable that this Administration will not be re-elected. Then it will be my duty to so co-operate with the President elect, as to save the Union between the election and the inauguration; as he will have secured his election on such ground that he can not possibly save it afterwards. [43]

McClellan did not win the election, however. In November, General William Tecumseh Sherman captured the Confederate stronghold of Atlanta, and the North's faith in Lincoln, as well as its fighting spirit, was renewed. McClellan bore the painful disappointment philosophically, writing, "For my country's sake I deplore the result—but the people have decided with their eyes wide open and I feel that a great weight is removed from my mind." [44]

Controversial in Death

After his defeat, George McClellan and his family spent time in Europe where, as his wife boasted, "they look upon him as *the* American general." [45] After several years of travel, he involved himself in various business and engineering projects, then, in 1878, was elected governor of New Jersey, where he gained a reputation as a careful executive. During his term he reduced taxes, reformed the militia, and encouraged the establishment of trade schools and local industry.

McClellan was only fifty-eight years old when he died of a heart attack on October 29, 1885. He was buried in Trenton, New Jersey. The general was widely mourned throughout the nation, but remained controversial even in death. One newspaper, the *New York World*, declared, "No general who fought in the war . . . was

Removed from Command

McClellan had heard rumors of his removal from command prior to the event, which occurred in November 1862. In his memoirs, McClellan's Own Story, *the general remembers the painful moment that marked the end of his military career.*

"Late at night I was sitting alone in my tent, writing to my wife. All the staff were asleep. Suddenly some one knocked upon the tent-pole, and, upon my invitation to enter there appeared [General Ambrose] Burnside and [Brigadier General Catharinus] Buckingham, both looking very solemn. I received them kindly and commenced conversation upon general subjects in the most unconcerned manner possible. After a few moments Buckingham said to Burnside: 'Well, general, I think we had better tell Gen. McClellan the object of our business.' I very pleasantly said that I should be glad to learn it. Whereupon Buckingham handed me the two orders of which he was the bearer. [One of them read as follows.]

Headquarters of the Army
Washington, Nov. 5, 1862

Maj.-Gen. McClellan, Commanding, etc.:

General: On receipt of the order of the President, sent herewith, you will immediately turn over your command to Maj.-Gen. Burnside, and repair to Trenton, N.J., reporting on your arrival at that place, by telegraph, for further orders.

Very respectfully, your obedient servant,

H. W. Halleck,
Gen.-in-Chief"

ever actuated by nobler sentiments and purer and more patriotic motives." The *New York Post* noted, "Probably no soldier who did so little fighting has ever had his qualities as a commander so minutely, and we may add, so fiercely discussed." [46]

McClellan was a great organizer, an efficient trainer of men, and a notable scholar of military history. In the end, however, he was too cautious to be a great field general. The nation, torn by war, recognized that and would not let him remain its leader.

CHAPTER 3

Reluctant Commander

To President Lincoln, the tall, friendly general with the distinctive side whiskers seemed the best man to replace George McClellan, who had been dismissed as head of the Army of the Potomac on November 5, 1862. Thirty-eight-year-old Ambrose Everett Burnside had been a friend of McClellan's since their days together at West Point. He was reportedly intelligent and well liked. Lincoln and Secretary of War Stanton hoped that he would be the fighter that McClellan was not.

Within three months, however, the country saw a different side of the likable general. Burnside's good nature masked characteristics that hindered his management of a force the size of the Army of the Potomac. Like McClellan before him and other Union generals who would follow, Burnside proved unable to fight war on the grand and bloody scale necessary to win.

Striking in appearance and congenial in demeanor, Ambrose Burnside replaced McClellan as commander of the Army of the Potomac in November 1862.

Early Days

Ambrose Burnside was born on May 23, 1824, in Liberty, Indiana, the fourth of nine children of Edghill and Pamelia Burnside. Burnside senior was a county court clerk who farmed to make ends meet, and as a boy, Ambrose often worked in his father's fields. He also had time to learn the basics of English and arithmetic in the one-room building that served as the community schoolhouse in Liberty. After completing his studies there, he was privately tutored by future governor Samuel Bigger, who found his student to be both honest and able.

In late 1840, sixteen years old and feeling pressured to earn his way in his large family, Burnside dropped out of school to become a tailor's apprentice. When his mother died the following spring, the young man opened his own business in Liberty, but to his dismay discovered that he could not bear the thought of spending his life sitting cross-legged on a tailor's bench.

His father came to his rescue. Although the elder Burnside could not afford to send his children to college, he did have a few connections with men in high places. Thanks to the combined recommendations of both Indiana's U.S. senators and members of the Indiana legislature, in March 1843, Ambrose was awarded a scholarship to attend the U.S. Military Academy at West Point.

For many a young man, the obligations of living up to his benefactors' expectations would have proven sobering. Burnside had a happy-go-lucky outlook, however, and although he did well in math at the academy, he regularly earned demerits for smoking, violating the uniform code, and talking while on duty. In the first year he earned 198 demerits—200 meant dismissal—and was ranked fourth from the bottom of his class in general conduct. A summer vacation spent on the family farm convinced him of the benefits of behaving and studying hard, and in 1847 he graduated eighteenth in his class of thirty-eight.

While stationed at Fort Adams, Rhode Island, Burnside met and married Mary Richmond Bishop, "a dainty creature who befriended people as easily as her husband," biographer William Marvel writes.[47] The couple had no children, but the six-foot, broad-shouldered Burnside served as a father figure to his brothers and sisters, especially after their father's death. A devoted husband, he also took time for his wife's relatives, caring for her mother as if she were his own.

Bad Timing and Poor Business Sense

In 1853 Burnside resigned from the service, borrowed money, and set to work establishing his own business, the Bristol Rifle Works, in Bristol, Rhode Island. There he designed, manufactured, and marketed a breech-loading rifle, that is, a long gun that was loaded near the trigger end of the muzzle rather than at its mouth. The guns were well made and an improvement over traditional rifles. They were also widely used during the Civil War, but in the 1850s Burnside found little market for them. His bad timing and poor business sense forced him to sell the business at a loss and give up everything to repay his investors. In 1858 he headed west. "I am now thrown upon the world with absolutely nothing," he wrote.[48] With the help of his friend George McClellan, he finally found work with the Illinois Central Railroad in Chicago.

A New Chapter

Three days after the assault on Fort Sumter in April 1861, Burnside received a telegram from the governor of Rhode Island, asking him to lead an infantry regiment from that state. Burnside kissed his wife good-bye and set out immediately for Providence. Within days of accepting his command, he had his men outfitted in smart uniforms of his own design (a reminder of his days as a tailor) and on their way to Washington. Shortly after the first Battle of Bull Run, during which Burnside saved his men from capture by leading them in an orderly retreat, the bewhiskered commander received news that he had been given a commission as brigadier general of volunteers. He was to serve under his old friend George McClellan, who was now commander of the Army of the Potomac.

Burnside took on his new commission enthusiastically, and soon he and McClellan devised a plan whereby he would lead an amphibious division of men down the coast of North Carolina against several Confederate strongholds. Concerned with every detail of the undertaking, during the following weeks Burnside gathered his troops, procured necessary ships, saw that his men had uniforms and guns, and, in the words of William Marvel, "gave all [his] correspondence his personal eye." [49]

Ambrose Burnside and soldiers from his Rhode Island regiment relax at their camp following the Battle of Bull Run.

Fighter and Hero

Burnside set out on his venture in the first week of January 1862. Despite storms, illness, and other hardships, his expedition of more than ten thousand men and almost one hundred vessels successfully traveled down the coast, reconnoitering and clashing with Confederates along the way. In a letter to George McClellan, dated March 15, Burnside wrote, "We've got New Berne, and I hope to have Fort Macon before long. I've followed your instructions to the letter, and have succeeded." [50] Shortly thereafter, he captured twenty-five hundred Confederates on Roanoke Island. This action, the first significant Union victory in many long, depressing months, established Burnside's reputation as a fighter and a hero. Historians note, however, that his well-armed men had heavily outnumbered the enemy.

Burnside's capture of parts of North Carolina not only earned him fame, it resulted in his promotion to major general of volunteers, a move that delighted his men. Burnside was highly popular with those in his command because he was good-tempered and often gave his officers wide discretionary powers. Burnside attended to details in other aspects of his work, but he constantly relied on the wisdom of his subordinates in battle, and generously did not blame them if they made poor decisions. William Marvel notes, "[Burnside's] greatest contributions to the expedition's vic-

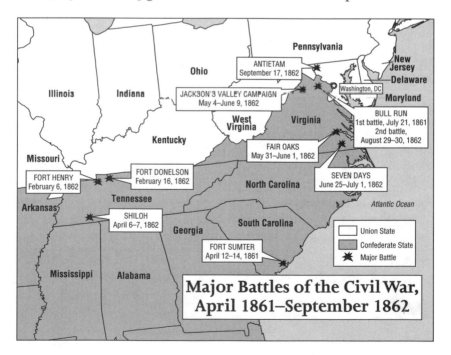

Major Battles of the Civil War, April 1861–September 1862

Too Many Details

Although not a gifted strategist, Burnside put much time and effort into planning his first expedition down the North Carolina coast as historian William Marvel describes in his biography, Burnside.

"Burnside's close supervision of his command amounted very nearly to a fault. While outfitting the expedition [to North Carolina], he saw personally to the specifications of the vessels, chartered them, and inspected them. Almost daily he made the rounds of the ships, seeing to the comfort and health of the men, reviewing the plans for landings and assaults, and consulting with his immediate subordinates. In battle he often delivered orders in person. All of these duties could have been assigned to staff officers. Attending personally to so many details did eliminate much opportunity for misunderstanding . . . but the disinclination to share the labor with his staff often caused him to overwork himself. At a higher level of command, that tendency could [and proved to] be dangerous."

tories seem to have been his moral courage, his exhaustive attention to administrative detail, and his readiness to rely upon—and credit—his subordinates' abilities."[51]

Burnside's weaknesses as a commander became apparent when he did not have competent subordinates or was forced to make tactical decisions on his own. Then he was nervous, uninspired, and prone to poor judgment. Such was the case during the Battle of Antietam in late September 1862. In that engagement, Burnside was slow in supporting McClellan, unwisely sent his men across a bridge to certain death under heavy enemy fire, and was responsible for many of the Union casualties, which exceeded twelve thousand.

Presidential Request

By the summer of 1862, President Lincoln was growing impatient with George McClellan, whose reluctance to fight was hampering the war effort. Thus, in July, he privately offered Burnside McClellan's position as head of the Army of the Potomac. Lincoln appreciated Burnside's success in what he had set out to do in North Carolina. In addition, Burnside was popular with his men, a quality lacking in other qualified generals such as George Meade and Joseph Hooker.

Burnside refused the offer. William Marvel describes, "Two humble sons of Midwestern pioneers faced each other across the desk, one gently probing, the other modestly shaking his head.

Union and Confederate forces meet at the Battle of Antietam. Burnside's poor decisions cost many lives during the frenzied engagement.

McClellan was the better general, Burnside argued, and only needed a fair opportunity to prove it."[52]

In early November, however, Lincoln replaced McClellan without discussion, again asking Burnside to take the command. Burnside at first refused, but this time the president strengthened his argument by holding up Joseph Hooker as his second choice. Lincoln's strategy worked. Burnside despised Hooker, and reluctantly accepted command of the Army of the Potomac, still feeling unfit for the heavy burden. He was not afraid to take responsibility, but he was convinced there were better leaders than he. The head of the army needed to be an expert judge of men's characters. He needed to think quickly, to delegate duties, and to be able to deal with a multitude of problems simultaneously. None of these qualities came naturally to Burnside. Marvel explains:

> Burnside not only judged men generously rather than well, he found it next to impossible to apportion staff labor and digest the resulting information with so extensive an organization. Worst of all, he was a slow thinker. He had no leisure for bounding in front of parading troops; . . . so seriously did he take his duties, he had no stomach for it either.[53]

Burnside also worried that McClellan loyalists would resent his advancement. "Little Mac" was so popular with his men that there was bound to be grumblings at his removal.

Burnside's fears proved real. A few troops were happy with his promotion. "We are well pleased with Burnside. Thank God for the prospect ahead now, our soldiers will fight as well under B. as McC," one testified.[54] But many of McClellan's men saw their new leader as an intruder. Rumors of mutiny abounded among his officers, and all problems and failures were blamed on Burnside.

Fredericksburg

Increasingly nervous and depressed, Burnside struggled with the new responsibilities he had been handed. In his opinion, the com-

---

An Honest and Humble Man

No man appeared better suited to command the Army of the Potomac in 1862 than genial, charismatic Ambrose Burnside. But Burnside's qualifications proved only skin deep, as historian T. Harry Williams points out in Lincoln and His Generals.

"People could not help liking Ambrose E. Burnside. His smile was charming, his manner was hearty, and his ways were winning. He cast a spell over most people when they met him. He was a handsome and striking figure of a man. About six feet in height, he was big in build. His large face was surrounded by heavy whiskers, which were almost the trademark of his appearance. In his dress, he was studiedly careless and informal. He liked to wear an undress uniform and a fatigue cap. When he rode before the troops, he wore large buckskin gauntlets and a loose pistol belt that allowed his holster to swing at his hip. He seemed dashing and brave, and he was. He also seemed to be very intelligent, but he was not. One keen observer said: You have to know Burnside some time before you realize there is not much behind his showy front. This was unjust. Burnside was an honest and a humble man. He was a good subordinate general. But he did not have the brains to command a large army. He had been right when he had twice before refused the command because he doubted his ability."

Despite his charisma and military experience, General Burnside lacked the tactical intelligence necessary for command.

mander of the Army of the Potomac needed a comprehensive plan by which he could crush the rebellion and bring an end to the war. Burnside had no such plan; his command of the expedition to North Carolina had been the extent of his creativity thus far. Nevertheless, he hastily drew up a strategy whereby he would march his army to Fredericksburg, Virginia, a key transportation center on the banks of the Rappahannock River. After taking Fredericksburg, he would proceed against Richmond. Lincoln supported the scheme, but pointed out that Burnside would have to move quickly if he were to get his army across the Rappahannock before winter floods made it impassable.

Burnside set out in good time, but he ran into delays. Pontoon bridges, which his men needed if they were to cross the Rappahannock quickly and en masse, had not arrived, and the general did not want to try to cross without them. Thus he delayed his attack for several weeks, and by then Lee had arrived and positioned his troops. Nevertheless, Burnside went ahead with his plans. Historian Bruce Catton observes, "He had said he would cross at Fredericksburg, and at Fredericksburg he would cross, even if destruction awaited him." [55]

"How Beautifully They Came On"

The Union advance finally began early on the cold morning of December 11, 1862, directly across from Fredericksburg. The fog was thick, but Lee's Confederates could see enough to begin firing on unarmed construction crews who were setting the bridges in place. Burnside promptly ordered his artillery to pound the city, hoping to clear some of the resistance.

By the end of the next day, the Federals had taken Fredericksburg, and the Confederates had retreated to the hills behind the town. There Lee seized the advantage. He dug in, stationing his guns and men where they could easily take aim during an assault. Hundreds huddled behind a sturdy stone wall that ran along the base of the hills and watched the Federal advance. "How beautifully they came on. Their bright bayonets glistening in the sunlight made the line look like a huge serpent of blue and steel," one Confederate observed. [56]

With the serpent in their sights, the Rebels opened fire, cutting down their enemies in enormous numbers. Soon, the ground was covered with bodies, as historian Bruce Catton describes:

> The fighting was sheer murder. Coming out from the town, Burnside's men crashed into the stone wall and were

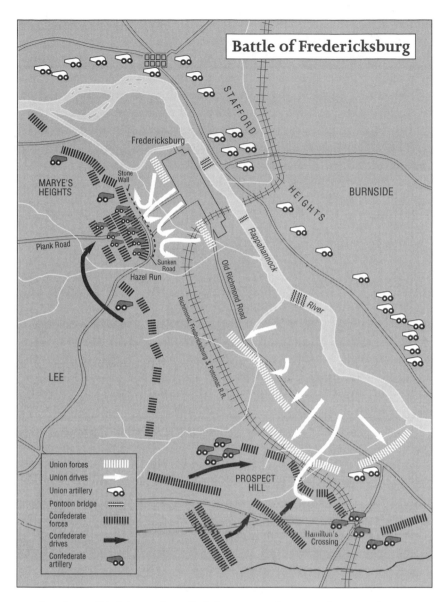

Battle of Fredericksburg

STAFFORD

Fredericksburg

Stone Wall

HEIGHTS

MARYE'S HEIGHTS

BURNSIDE

Rappahannock

Plank Road

Sunken Road

Hazel Run

Old Richmond Road

River

Richmond, Fredericksburg & Potomac R.R.

LEE

Union forces
Union drives
Union artillery
Pontoon bridge
Confederate forces
Confederate drives
Confederate artillery

PROSPECT HILL

Hamilton's Crossing

broken. Division after division moved up to the attack . . . to be cut and broken and driven back by a storm of fire; for hour after hour they attacked, until all the plain was stained with the blue bodies that had been thrown on it, and not one armed Yankee ever reached even the foot of the hill.[57]

Despite the bloodbath, Burnside did not order retreat. If he could take the heights, he reasoned, his men would not have died in vain. It was a futile hope. The Federals were beaten back fourteen times during disastrous assaults that continued for hours. At the end of the day, victory lay with the Confederates. When he finally saw how great his losses were, Burnside broke down and wept. "Oh! oh those men! oh, those men!" he cried, pointing to the battlefield. "Those men over there! I am thinking of them all the time." [58]

Even tortured by grief, however, Burnside was determined to avenge his losses. At a meeting with his subordinates, he desperately proposed leading a bayonet charge into the hills the next morning. His officers convinced him it would be foolish and counseled retreat. Finally Burnside agreed. Marvel writes:

> With tears running into those famous whiskers [Burnside] dictated orders to abandon Fredericksburg altogether. A miserable rainstorm helped to muffle the sound of his retreat, and by the dawn of December 16 the entire Army of the Potomac sat on the other side of the Rappahannock. The bloodstained bridges were gone. [59]

Relieved of Command

Union casualties for the Battle of Fredericksburg were eventually tallied at over twelve thousand, and Burnside was widely criticized for his failures there. "Little Mac's friends are jubilant," said one officer. "The title of the battle is Burnside's slaughterhouse," quipped an enlisted man. [60] Burnside himself took full responsibility for the disaster. "For the failure in the attack I am responsible, as the extreme gallantry, courage and endurance shown by [my men] was never excelled, and would have carried the points had it been possible." [61]

General Burnside issues orders during the Battle of Fredericksburg. Burnside's failure at Fredericksburg would ultimately cost him his command.

In following weeks, criticism of Burnside circulated through the army, desertions increased, and insubordination among his officers grew. The harassed general's efforts to deal with the latter proved to be his last acts as commander of the Army of the Potomac. In January he drew up General Order Number 8, which recommended the dismissal of his strongest critics, Generals Hooker, Brooks, Newton, and Cochrane. Since

Burnside had no real authority to remove these men, he turned to Lincoln for support.

Lincoln could not comply. Regretfully he told the general that he, Burnside, was being relieved of command and Hooker put in his place. The order was a bitter humiliation, but Burnside's responsibilities had become almost unbearably heavy. He accepted his reassignment to the Department of the Ohio. Five months later, he received news that Hooker, too, had been reassigned, having proved to be equally ill suited as a leader.

A Tragic Decision

Following his months with the Army of the Potomac, Burnside went on to participate in other campaigns, building his reputation as a dedicated officer of solid worth. In March 1863, as head of the Department of the Ohio, a command encompassing Michigan, Ohio, Indiana, Illinois, and most of Kentucky, he was forced to deal with strong hostility toward the government in the southwestern part of the region. Such hostility was due partly to public resentment of the government's draft law and partly to Democratic opposition to the Republican administration.

Burnside demonstrated his loyalty to the Union by issuing an order that stated in part, "It must be distinctly understood that treason, expressed or implied, will not be tolerated in this department." [62] When one man defiantly denounced the government, Burnside had him arrested and imprisoned.

His loyal service notwithstanding, in mid-1864 Burnside made another decision that led to the deaths of thousands of men and occasioned his resignation from the army. The event took place on the outskirts of Petersburg, Virginia, a Confederate-held city then besieged by the Union army. Burnside, serving under General George Meade, commander of the Army of the Potomac, was a part of this siege force.

Shortly after June when the siege began, one of Burnside's subordinates, Lieutenant Colonel Henry Pleasants, came to him with a plan by which Union troops might penetrate Petersburg's defenses. The plan involved destroying a small fort that sat less than a hundred yards beyond Union lines in Confederate territory. Many of the men in the 48th Pennsylvania Infantry had been coal miners before the war. Pleasants himself was a mining engineer. He pointed out that they could easily tunnel under the fort and blow it up, thus creating an opening in the Confederate lines.

Burnside gave his consent, and before the end of the month the Pennsylvanians were at work. By mid-July, the tunnel was all but finished. Burnside carefully charted the assault that would follow the explosion and chose the troops to lead the attack.

Battle of the Crater

At dawn on Saturday, July 30, 1864, Pleasants lit the fuse that would set off the four tons of powder packed into the Confederate end of the five-hundred-foot tunnel. The enormity of the explosion that followed was terrible, taking everyone by surprise. General Horace Porter, who was standing nearby, remembered:

> Suddenly there was a shock like that of an earthquake, accompanied by a dull, muffled roar. Then there rose two hundred feet in the air great volumes of earth in the shape of a mighty inverted cone. . . . The mass seemed to be suspended for an instant in the heavens; then there descended great blocks of clay, rock, sand, timber, guns, carriages, and men whose bodies exhibited every form of mutilation.[63]

As soon as the rubble stopped falling, the first division of Union soldiers stormed their way forward, yelling and cheering. Encountering only minimal resistance, some raced around the enormous crater, which measured about seventy feet wide, two hundred fifty feet long, and thirty feet deep. Others charged down into its depths.

These latter troops soon made two unwelcome discoveries. First, no commanding officer was present to direct their advance. Their leader, General James Ledlie, had retreated with a bottle of liquor to a bombproof shelter behind the lines. Second, the walls of the crater were sheer and crumbling, and no one had thought to provide ladders. The men were trapped at the bottom, exposed to enemy fire.

Following conventional army tactics, Burnside hurriedly sent in backup troops, which included a division of Negroes. By then, the Confederates had rallied and were firing down into the hole. The result was panic and wholesale slaughter. "The troops in the Crater . . . degenerated into a mob, dense and disorganized; they could do almost nothing to defend themselves," Marvel writes.[64]

As he had done at Fredericksburg, Burnside allowed the melee to continue for hours, again hoping that his men could turn defeat into victory. He belatedly gave the order to withdraw sometime around noon. By then, the hot sun was baking the crater, and men were choking and begging for water in the suffocating dust. As the Federals prepared a disordered retreat, the Confederates charged. Half of Burnside's men successfully made the dash to safety; others surrendered and were marched ignominiously away.

Burnside later estimated the number of Union casualties during the battle to be forty-five hundred. Even without knowing their exact losses, the Union camp realized by nightfall that it had witnessed one of the most stupendous failures of the war. One Union soldier remembered, "The work and expectations of almost two months have been blasted. . . . Fifteen minutes changed it all. . . . Few officers can be found this evening who have not drowned their sorrows in the flowing bowl [gotten drunk]." [65]

Burden of Command

Burnside unhappily accepted command of the Army of the Potomac in November 1862. From that moment, he bore an almost unbearably heavy burden of responsibility, which depressed him to the point of illness, as William Marvel describes in Burnside.

"Due at least partly to his disinclination to delegate authority, Burnside had been working feverishly at all hours since General Buckingham consigned him that accursed appointment. General Howard noted that Burnside's first two nights as army commander were almost sleepless. Daniel Larned, his faithful secretary, complained that Burnside worked continually, day and night, sleeping little, ignoring his personal health, and Larned ominously mentioned at one point, 'The general has been sick since he took command.' While McClellan had screened himself from interruptions with a headquarters guard, Burnside scorned such pretensions and so suffered from an endless cycle of importuning visitors who distracted him and disturbed his rest. The toll is evident in his photographs. The images of Burnside before he took command show determination and vigor; photographs taken afterward reveal a droopy sort of resignation, the eyes tired and dull, the famous whiskers heavily salted with grey."

Burnside (center), shown here shortly after assuming command of the Union army, suffered from severe depression during his stressful appointment.

No Longer of Service

After the Battle of the Crater, a court of inquiry called by George Meade found Burnside and his officers responsible for the tragedy outside Petersburg. Other leaders of the Army of the Potomac had exhibited faults and weaknesses that prolonged the war and increased the bloodshed, but Burnside was conspicuous for his ineptitude and the number of lives he needlessly sacrificed.

By early September when the court brought in its decision, Burnside had left Washington to spend time with his family. At the end of that period, he optimistically notified Grant that he was awaiting orders for his next assignment. That assignment did not materialize. In the spring of 1865, he humbly telegraphed the secretary of war, "If I can be of any service to General Grant or General Sherman as a subordinate commander or aide-de-camp, or as a bearer of dispatches from you to either of them, I am quite ready." [66] The secretary ignored the telegraph.

Finally accepting the inevitable, Ambrose Burnside sent in his resignation from the army on April 14, 1865. On that same day, Lincoln was assassinated.

Postwar Career

Burnside's natural optimism and good spirits revived somewhat after his return to private life. His military career had ended, but he discovered he could serve the public in other ways. Still popular with constituents in his home state, he was elected governor of Rhode Island in 1866, then served as U.S. senator from 1875 to 1881. In 1876, after years of poor health, Mary Burnside died, taking to her grave much of Burnside's joy in life. Nevertheless, he continued to work until his retirement in 1881. From that time, he led the life of a gentleman farmer, overseeing his property in Rhode Island from the back of Major, the high-stepping bobtail grey that had carried him faithfully through the war.

Burnside died of a heart attack on September 13, 1881, at the age of fifty-four. He was buried in Providence, Rhode Island. One of his eulogists, Reverend Augustus Woodbury, remembered the words the general spoke shortly after his defeat at Fredericksburg. "I have simply to do my duty. I can safely leave any claim that I have to the judgement of future years and the justice of my fellow countrymen." [67]

Ironically, those countrymen placed Burnside among the ranks of others who attempted to lead the nation to victory and failed.

CHAPTER 4

The Beast

Much attention is paid to Civil War generals who led armies, risked their lives on the battlefield, and fought for the cause in which they believed. Other generals, however, had less visible roles in the war, serving as military governors who enforced martial law in locales defeated and then occupied by Union troops.

The most well known and controversial military governor was General Benjamin Franklin Butler, a Massachusetts lawyer who gained notoriety while overseeing New Orleans in 1862. Although Butler was admired by some as one of the smartest men of his time, many of his enemies dubbed him "the Beast," and claimed that he was the most unscrupulous, cold-blooded man to rise to power in the war.

Life's Bitter Lessons

Benjamin Franklin Butler was born in Deerfield, New Hampshire, on November 5, 1818. His father was a sailor and an adventurer, serving as a privateer (plundering British ships for the U.S. government) in the War of 1812, sailing under the Bolivian flag after the war, then becoming a trader in the West Indies, where he died of yellow fever when his son was only four.

Raised by his mother and older sister, Butler was thin and undersized as a boy. His intellect was enormous, however. By the age of four he had mastered the alphabet and the basics of spelling, and within the year was an avid reader, preferring books to sports.

Controversial general Benjamin Butler was both renowned for his intelligence and denounced for his cold-hearted nature.

His favorite novel was *Robinson Crusoe*, although at his mother's insistence he read an equal number of pages in the New Testament as well. To please her, Butler memorized entire passages, which he remembered all his life.

Butler's memory was powerful, and his interest in learning insatiable. He spent hours in the town library, reading books on ancient history. Although he could not comprehend all he read, he remembered the facts, just as he remembered everything he was taught at elementary school, Exeter Academy in New Hampshire, and later at Lowell High School in Massachusetts. His paternal grandmother, an eighty-year-old pioneer feminist who visited her daughter-in-law regularly, also helped mold his thinking as she discoursed at the dinner table about men's unfairness to women.

Despite his puny body and studious disposition, Butler was a fighter who often won his skirmishes with other boys in the neighborhood. He also developed a reputation for lying and trickery. Perhaps in hopes that a change of locale would benefit her son, the younger Mrs. Butler moved her family to Lowell, Massachusetts, in 1828. There Butler continued his schooling. By the age of eighteen, however, his heart was set on a military career.

Butler's mother tried hard to gain a place for him at the U.S. Military Academy at West Point, but the congressman to whom she applied smoothly dismissed her request. Historian Robert Holzman writes, "Ben was horribly disappointed, but this setback taught him something he was never to forget: political influence is the key to many desirable things. He also acquired at this moment a lasting contempt for all those who *had* been to West Point."[68]

Still smarting from the West Point rejection, Butler finished his formal studies at Colby College in Maine, and then, at the age of twenty, went on a four-month sea voyage to build up his ninety-seven-pound body. He returned to Lowell twenty-five pounds heavier, with his mind set on a profession: the practice of law. Law was the path to power and riches, two things that were important to Butler all his life.

Pathway to Power

Butler's intelligence, near-photographic memory, and habit of working hard soon earned him a place as a first class Massachusetts attorney. His clientele was varied. He represented the rich as well as working people who could not afford good lawyers. He drew up patent specifications for Elias Howe's new invention, the sewing machine. At the age of twenty-seven, he became the youngest man to argue a case before the U.S. Supreme Court. It was an action on behalf of John Sutter, on whose property in California gold was first discovered. A fellow attorney wrote of Butler in pre–Civil War days, "He is earnest and zealous. He compromises nothing. If he feels anger, he doesn't smother it. . . . And, on the whole, it cannot be doubted that he is the most skillful lawyer, in many respects, now living in New England." [69]

Despite his zeal, Butler never hesitated to disregard the spirit of the law to gain victory, and he made many enemies in and out of his practice. When a client was charged with larceny—the theft of a key from a door preparatory to burglary—Butler won an acquittal by establishing that the theft was of real estate (the key being part of the door at the time) and so could not be larceny, which is theft of personal property. When his home town of Lowell passed an ordinance requiring all dogs on the street to be muzzled, Butler's dog wore a muzzle on its tail. "He liked audacious surprises. He was seldom content to try a simple case in a simple way," grumbled one of his opponents. [70]

Immersed in the Law

Few men could match the energy and stamina that propelled Benjamin Butler to prominence in Massachusetts and later in the war. In his biography Stormy Ben Butler, *Robert S. Holzman describes the schedule Butler followed while studying and practicing law as a young man.*

"[Butler] commenced reading law at seven every morning, stopping at noon to eat. Before one o'clock he was back at his books for another five-hour stint, after which he would take time off to eat again. At seven o'clock in the evening he was back in the office, where he would remain until ten. Then he would rent a horse and ride for a few hours, reciting poetry aloud. For two years this schedule was not varied, unless Butler was so engrossed in a problem that he could not leave the office at ten; on occasion he did not call for his horse until midnight. . . .

As a young attorney, Butler worked the eighteen-hour day that he had pursued as a clerk. . . . For several years his only diversion was military exercises with the City Guard, which later became a part of the state militia. He joined as a private, but in time he was to serve in every rank up to the top. The young lawyer apparently enjoyed the military pageantry, and upon one occasion he sent a note calling for his full-dress uniform: 'Gauntlet Gloves . . . Full Dress Sword Sash Spurs Cap belt Pompon and *all.*'"

Butler was interested not only in law, but politics as well. In 1860 he served as a delegate to the Democratic National Convention, where he ignored his state's instructions to vote for Stephen B. Douglas, whose policies he disliked. The majority of delegates could not agree on a candidate and had to vote repeatedly, so Butler craftily cast his ballot for unpopular Jefferson Davis. He knew that Davis could not win, but hoped for a deadlocked convention that would eventually compromise on Butler's personal favorite, James Guthrie of Kentucky. Douglas eventually won the nomination, and Butler had to return home and explain his defection to a booing crowd.

Despite all his scheming, Butler found time for romance. He was not a handsome man—one observer described him as a "cross-eyed cuttlefish" [71]—but he was fascinating enough to capture the heart of beautiful Sarah Hildreth, who left her career as a professional actress to marry him in 1844. The couple was able to build a luxurious home in Lowell and live in style, using the proceeds of Butler's many shrewd business investments.

Troublesome Amateur

When war broke out in 1861, Butler's quick wits and expanding political connections helped him secure a position as brigadier general of the Massachusetts volunteers. Members of the regular army protested his high rank, pointing out that he had no formal military training. Ignoring such objections Butler had his men provisioned and on their way to Washington within a week of the shelling of Fort Sumter. They earned Lincoln's personal thanks for being the first troops to come to the defense of the capital.

Soon after arriving in Washington, Butler was awarded a new command, the Department of Annapolis in Maryland. The assignment presented few challenges, however, so with time on his hands, the general decided to capture and occupy nearby Baltimore, a Confederate-held city. His efforts were successful, but his army superiors were outraged at his independent and autocratic methods. General in chief Winfield Scott admonished Butler, "Your hazardous occupation of Baltimore was made without my knowledge, and, of course, without my approbation. It is a godsend that it was without a conflict of arms." [72]

Unlike General Scott, Lincoln believed it was better to make use of Butler's talents than to quarrel with him. On the day Scott wired his rebuke, the president promoted Butler to major general and offered him an assignment at Fortress Monroe, a strategic fortification overlooking traffic on navigable rivers in Virginia and North Carolina. Butler accepted the assignment. It was not the

A runaway slave is captured in accordance with the Fugitive Slave Act of 1850. General Butler showed compassion for runaways by giving them jobs rather than returning them to slavery.

most challenging of missions, but he was confident that some problem worthy of his talents would come along soon. He would be ready to deal with it when it did.

"Contraband of War"

The challenge Butler was looking for materialized one day in May 1861, in the form of three runaway slaves seeking protection at the fort. The problem of dealing humanely with runaway slaves had been bedeviling the North for some time. The Fugitive Slave Act of 1850 decreed that Northerners were obliged to return slaves to their masters, but many Northerners were abolitionists, and the act was repugnant to them. Butler was not a rampant abolitionist, but he did not support slavery, and he did not hesitate to ignore a law in which he did not believe. He put the three escapees to work at the fort rather than returning them to their master.

Predictably, his action was challenged by the outraged Confederate owner, who discovered his property and demanded its return. Butler's resourceful legal mind quickly came up with an answer. He calmly pointed out that, having seceded, Southern states were

Air of Authority

Benjamin Butler's critics often used his appearance to color their articles, seldom failing to mention his stoutness and his squinting, slightly crossed eyes. One such article, penned by a journalist at about the time of Butler's occupation of Baltimore, is included in Robert Holzman's Stormy Ben Butler.

"I found him clothed in a gorgeous military uniform adorned with rich gold embroidery. His rotund form, his squinting eye, and the peculiar puff of his cheeks made him look a little grotesque. Only a person much more devoid of a sense of humor than I was, would have failed to notice that General Butler thoroughly enjoyed his position of power, which, of course, was new to him, and that he keenly appreciated its theatrical possibilities. . . . While we were conversing, officers entered from time to time to make reports or to ask for orders. Nothing could have been more striking than the air of authority with which the General received them, and the tone of curt peremptoriousness [arrogance] . . . with which he gave his instructions. And, after every such scene, he looked around with a sort of triumphant gaze, as if to assure himself that the bystanders were duly impressed."

A Civil War–era photograph of General Benjamin Butler, who endured much ridicule for his stout appearance and squinting eyes.

technically foreign nations. According to the law, the federal government had no obligation to return slaves to foreign nations. "I shall hold these Negroes as contraband of war," he informed the Confederate officer who, under a flag of truce, had come for the slaves. "If [their owner] will come into the fort and take the oath of allegiance to the United States he shall have his Negroes." [73]

The phrase "contraband of war" (war material which by law could be seized by a government) caught the attention of Northerners, who recognized it as a way of cutting through legalities and ignoring the Fugitive Slave Law. Slaves, too, saw it as a means of freedom, and soon almost one thousand fugitives had made their way to Fortress Monroe.

Operation New Orleans

When Butler's duty at Fortress Monroe ended after three months, his superiors again realized that it was dangerous to leave the wily and ambitious general unoccupied. Thus in February 1862, they asked him to be part of a joint expedition with the navy to capture and occupy New Orleans. The Louisiana city was of great military importance to the North, since it was a center of foreign trade and also a gateway for shipping on the Mississippi River.

The navy took the city of 168,000 people in April, and Butler and his men entered it shortly thereafter. They quickly discovered that the city's populace was exceedingly hostile and had no intention of submitting quietly to Union occupation. One observer wrote, "As soon . . . as they saw Butler, and the triumphant and pompous strut of the Yankees, and heard the music, the indignation of the *canaille* [mob] knew no bounds; they knew no language too gross to accost him with." [74] The mayor himself demanded that Butler and his men treat citizens with consideration, contending that New Orleans was not a captured city.

General Butler was detested throughout the South for his ruthless governing of captured cities.

Butler, who wasted no time with diplomacy, bluntly cut to the heart of the matter.

> New Orleans is a conquered city. . . . Did you open your arms and bid us welcome? Would you not expel us if you could? . . . I therefore proclaim martial law. . . . I warn you that if a shot is fired from any house, . . . and if I can discover the perpetrator of the deed, the place that knows him now shall know him no more forever.[75]

Administering a hostile city was a difficult job for any military governor, but Butler was particularly ruthless in convincing the citizens of New Orleans that they could not lightly disregard his orders. He arrested and hanged a man who had torn down a U.S. flag and dragged it through the streets. He ordered shop owners to open their doors and sell their goods to Federal soldiers, and when one merchant refused, Butler seized his property and sold it at auction. Owners who propped their doors partly open as a gesture of defiance were fined. Butler also imprisoned a contractor who refused to work for the army.

Butler did not focus only on those who rebelled against Union occupation, however. He went after criminals of all kinds and, because

Despite his harsh treatment of rebellious Southerners, Benjamin Butler displayed the utmost kindness for slaves who flocked to the Union army for protection.

of his tough crime-fighting measures, the city soon became safer than it had been before the war. Not even Union soldiers escaped punishment if they deserved it. Breaking up a burglary ring in the city, Butler ordered five members of the gang executed. One of them had formerly been second officer on Butler's personal command vessel.

Black Regiments

Butler's antislavery views hardened during his tenure in New Orleans, probably because he saw the conditions under which slaves lived in the South. As governor of the city, Butler improved conditions for blacks, worked to ensure that all were fed and housed, and provided many with jobs. He also granted them such unheard of equalities as full rights in court, and full access to public transit systems.

Butler was also one of the first Union generals who dared to make use of blacks as soldiers. On occupying New Orleans, he had needed troop reinforcements and so recruited "free colored" men for black regiments, despite widespread belief that Negroes were not capable of fighting. Later he welcomed all Negroes into his regiments, to their great satisfaction. "Will the slave fight? If

Southern women snub a Union soldier in the captured city of Richmond, Virginia. General Butler refused to tolerate such contemptuous behavior in New Orleans; his dreaded "Woman Order" put an end to prominent displays of disdain.

any man asks you, tell him no. But if anyone asks you will a Negro fight, tell him yes," said one black soldier.[76]

The "Woman Order"

Although Ben Butler represented law and order in New Orleans, citizens there fumed under his harsh dictates. Women who were passionately devoted to the Confederate cause regularly went out of their way to express loathing of the city's occupiers. They made sneering and sarcastic remarks under their breath. They pointedly left shops, offices, and even church if a Union soldier entered. They twitched aside their skirts to avoid contamination when passing Union troops on the street. Holzman writes, "One patriotic woman twirled her skirts so violently to express disdain . . . that she fell in the gutter."[77] In the most outrageous incident, someone emptied her chamber pot out a window over a soldier's head.

In his usual uncompromising style, Butler responded to the escalating problem by issuing what became known as the "Woman Order," which stated:

It is ordered, that hereafter, when any female shall, by word, gesture, or movement, insult or show contempt for any officer or soldier of the United States, she shall be regarded and held liable to be treated as a woman of the town plying her avocation.[78]

In other words, women who drew attention to themselves and acted like unrefined prostitutes were to be treated as such.

When Southerners heard of Butler's order, they were outraged, assuming that it would now be legal for Union soldiers to rape and assault Southern women at will. The governor of Louisiana called Butler a "panderer to lust and a desecrator of virtue."[79] A Confederate newspaper printed an editorial entitled "An Appeal to Every Southern Soldier" and begged, "Do not leave your women to the mercy of this merciless foe!"[80] One Confederate entrepreneur did brisk business selling chamber pots with the general's picture inside.

Justice for All

The Woman Order did not initiate the wave of abuse that Southerners feared. Instead, it curbed the insults and, along with Butler's other stern measures, helped restore order to the city. It also gave Butler time to focus on other issues that badly needed his attention.

First, New Orleans faced a food crisis. Most supplies had gone to the Confederate army; the rest were being sold at inflated prices by war profiteers. Butler assessed a special tax on the city's wealthy businessmen "for the relief of their destitute and starving neighbors" and used the money to purchase food.[81] He also confiscated goods from nearby plantations and Confederate warehouses, and sold it at low prices to ensure that the poor were fed first.

Predictably, this relief project drew protests from businessmen and foreign diplomats, who resented Butler's high-handed methods as much as the tax. There were other complaints as well. Butler required foreign citizens to take a loyalty oath or leave the country. He imprisoned the head of a French champagne company whom he suspected of carrying treasonable letters. He confiscated sugar intended for export to Europe. The grievances were so numerous and, at times, so petty, that one newspaper wrote:

If Gen. Butler rides up street, the consuls are sure to come in a body, and protest that he did not ride down. If he smokes a pipe in the morning, a deputation calls upon him in the evening to know why he did not smoke a cigar. If he drinks coffee, they will send some crude messenger with a note asking . . . why he did not drink tea.[82]

Yellow Fever

Butler not only dealt with crime, rebellion, hunger, and foreign relations, he fought disease in the city as well. Yellow fever regularly plagued New Orleans; it was common for 10 percent of the population to die of the illness every year. Butler rightly assumed that the fever was likely to strike hard at his men, who had never been exposed and had little resistance.

The general did not know that the disease is due to a virus, passed through the bite of a mosquito, but he had heard that a strict quarantine of ships from the Caribbean reduced the number of fever victims. He therefore imposed a forty-day quarantine on all ships from that region and directed port authorities to keep a sharp eye out for sick sailors.

He also began a cleanup of the city, since its dirtier sections were usually hardest hit. He hired men to clean canals, flush sewers and drains, clean streets, and repaint houses. He set up a garbage collection service, and forbade littering of any kind. One man who tested the law by throwing a crumpled piece of paper on the street was sent to jail for three months.

Destitute residents of New Orleans rush to receive food rations provided by General Butler's administration.

Predictably, Southerners complained that such precautions were too strict, or were hopeless measures against an unknown killer. Nevertheless, at the end of a year, only two cases of fever had been reported in the city, and those two were attributed to a ship's captain who had lied about an earlier landing at a fever-infested port.

Outlaw and Felon

Ben Butler's approach to governing was harsh, but in many ways he proved a conscientious overseer of New Orleans. Other aspects of his behavior, particularly many of his business dealings, were less admirable. He took part in some commercial transactions that appeared to profit him personally. For instance, rather than fill empty Union troop ships with sand as ballast on their return trip north, he purchased sugar cheaply and had the ships filled with it. When the ships arrived at their destination, Butler sold the sugar for a considerable profit. He also secured for his brother Andrew the opportunity to make money by buying cheap Southern commodities such as cotton cloth and sugar and shipping them north for sale at a high price.

Near the end of his appointment in New Orleans, Northerners and Southerners alike began to suspect General Butler of unscrupulous business dealings.

Though nothing could be proven against Butler, including allegations that he had helped finance the deals, his closeness to Andrew, an obvious speculator, made even Northerners critical. Senator Garret Davis of Massachusetts accused the general of conspiring with his brother to "seize abandoned property in Louisiana for private gains." [83] A special investigative agent of the U.S. Treasury observed, "It is not proper that the brother of the commanding General should devote himself to such an object. It leads to the belief that the General himself is interested. . . . The effect is bad." [84]

Butler's suspect transactions coupled with his despotic behavior so infuriated Southerners that Confederate president Jefferson

Davis finally issued a proclamation declaring the general an outlaw. Davis wrote,

> I, Jefferson Davis, President of the Confederate States of America, and in their name, do pronounce and declare that said Benjamin F. Butler to be a felon, deserving of capital punishment. . . . I do order that . . . in the event of his capture, the officer in charge of the capturing force do cause him to be immediately executed by hanging.[85]

Davis's order was never carried out, and Butler was relieved of his New Orleans command in December 1862 for reasons he was never able to discover. He left the city as he had entered it—as a conqueror with the power of life and death in his hands. His farewell address to the citizens conveyed that spirit:

> I have not been too harsh. I might have smoked you to death in caverns as were the Covenanters of Scotland by a royal British general, or roasted you like the people of Algiers were roasted by the French. . . . You might have been blown from the mouths of cannon as were the sepoys of Delhi,—and yet kept within the rules of civilized war as practiced by the most polished and hypocritical capitals of Europe. But I have not done so.[86]

Inept in Battle

After New Orleans, Butler was given command of the Army of the James, serving under Ulysses S. Grant. Grant found him to be an inept field general with little understanding of strategy or tactics. He was quarrelsome, unable to manage his men, slow to attack, and quick to retreat. In a memo to Washington, Grant wrote:

> There is want of knowledge how to execute, and particularly a prejudice against him as commander, that operates against his usefulness. . . . General Butler, not being a soldier by education or experience, is in the hands of his subordinates in the execution of all operations military.[87]

In January 1865, fed up with Butler's ignorant blundering, Grant directed him to return to Massachusetts and await further orders. Grant had not taken such action before, since Butler's influence with Lincoln and other important politicians made him a dangerous enemy. Rumormongers also suggested that Butler had damaging information about Grant—perhaps regarding his bouts of drinking—which he could use for blackmail if Grant moved against him. Butler did not retaliate after his removal, however, and Grant wrote generously of the bellicose general in his memoirs. "General Butler certainly gave his very earnest support to the war; and he gave his own best efforts personally to the suppression of the rebellion." [88]

Missed Opportunity

In 1864, with national elections drawing near and the war showing no signs of conclusion, dissatisfied radicals from both Republican and Democratic parties turned to Ben Butler as a possible presidential candidate. They saw him as a man of action and a leader who would tolerate no nonsense from the South. Lincoln himself recognized that the general, a war veteran and a Democrat, would be a dangerous opponent and asked him to be his vice presidential running mate in the coming campaign.

Butler, who disliked playing second fiddle to anyone, flatly refused. "Tell him I would not quit the field to be Vice-President even with himself as President, unless he gives me bond [assurance] . . . that he will die or resign within three months after his inauguration." [89] The words came back to haunt Butler when Lincoln was assassinated, just six weeks into his second term. Ironically, the general had passed up his chance to attain the power and position of which he had always dreamed. He had only himself to blame when Andrew Johnson became seventeenth president of the United States in April 1865.

Radical to the End

Butler's postwar career remained as eventful and turbulent as it had been prior to the conflict. In 1866 he ran for Congress and was elected. Though formerly a Demo-

After the war Benjamin Butler was elected to Congress, where he fought for the rights of the working class and for women.

crat, he joined the Radical Republicans, taking part in impeachment proceedings against President Andrew Johnson in 1868. While in office he identified himself with the working class, pushing for fair labor practices, safer working conditions, an end to monopolies, and the right to vote for women. In his spare time he practiced law, set up farms on which Negro families could work as sharecroppers, and built two new homes, one in Washington, the other overlooking a bay in Massachusetts.

In 1871 Butler began a protracted campaign to become governor of Massachusetts. Not even his beloved wife's death from throat cancer in 1876 broke his resolve. He finally succeeded in 1882, after switching parties yet again in order to be elected as a Democrat. During his term he continued to push for workers' rights. He also appointed a Negro, George L. Ruffin, and an Irish Catholic, Michael J. McCafferty, to be the first minority judges in Massachusetts. Because most of the state's leaders were Republicans, however, the majority of Butler's appointments and legislation were not passed.

After his retirement from politics at the age of sixty-six, Butler continued to practice law, trying cases in the Supreme Court until shortly before his death. In the end, his reputation alone helped him win victories. "They will settle on your terms when you tell them I have the case," he assured one client.[90]

Benjamin Butler died on January 11, 1893, of severe pneumonia, contracted after he had stood in the rain at a friend's funeral. He was buried in Lowell, Massachusetts. In the *New York Sun*, journalist Charles A. Dana called him "the most original, the most American, and the most picturesque character in our public life." [91] No doubt Butler would have been proud of that summation.

CHAPTER 5

Unconditional Surrender

By 1863 the nation had been at war for two years, and President Abraham Lincoln was still looking for a general who could defeat Robert E. Lee and bring the conflict to a close. He had given several men a chance—McClellan, Pope, Burnside, Hooker, and Meade. All had come up short.

Still, Lincoln was not without hope. He had one more general in mind, a mild-mannered man who had been fighting Confederates in the West since the war began. A man who looked like "a dumpy, slouchy little subaltern [low ranking officer]." [92] A man who was not afraid to fight.

Lincoln hoped that Ulysses S. Grant would be the person to end the war so the nation could reunite and begin the work of healing its wounds.

Ulysses S. Grant, who gained military expertise from the war rather than books, would ultimately secure a Northern victory.

An Unremarkable Beginning

Nothing in Ulysses Grant's early life indicated that he would become a renowned military leader when the nation went to war. Grant was born in Point Pleasant, Ohio, on April 27, 1822, the son of Jesse and Hannah Simpson Grant, who named him Hiram Ulysses. Grant was a sensitive boy with a love for horses that made him hate his father's tannery business, where aged horses were slaughtered for their skins. Rather than working there, he did a multitude of chores and

"No Glitter or Parade"

Civilians who saw Ulysses Grant off the battlefield often searched in vain for some visible hint of the qualities that made him a successful commander. F. M. Pixley, a visitor to Grant's camp in June 1864, saw only a pleasant, slightly abstracted man in a blue coat who could pass for a country storekeeper or a businessman. Pixley's description of the general is included in William S. McFeely's biography Grant.

"At the evening mess table I met Gen. Grant, and after a very hasty meal, I watched him for an hour as he sat by the camp fire. He is a small man, with a square resolute thinking face. He sat silent among the gentlemen of his staff, and my first impression was that he was moody, dull and unsocial. I afterwards found him pleasant, genial and agreeable. He keeps his own counsel, padlocks his mouth, while his countenance in battle or repose . . . indicates nothing—that is gives no expression of his feelings and no evidence of his intentions. . . . He has a habit of whittling with a small knife. He cuts a small stick into small chips, making nothing. It is evidently a mere occupation of the fingers, his mind all the while intent upon other things. Among men he is nowise noticeable. There is no glitter or parade about him. To me he seems but an earnest business man."

The mild-mannered countenance of Ulysses Grant gave no indication of his prowess as a commander.

"all the work done with horses," as he later recalled.[93] This was nothing more than handling the teams used for plowing and hauling endless wagonloads of firewood used at home and in the tannery, but it was satisfying just the same. Grant was never known for spectacular riding; he simply loved horses, and was easily able to handle high-spirited animals when other men could not.

In addition to his chores, Grant went to school regularly in Georgetown, Ohio, where the family moved in 1823. In 1836, at the age of fourteen, he went to stay for a year with relatives in Maysville,

Kentucky, and attended the Richardson and Rand Academy there. Grant was particularly good in arithmetic and enjoyed reading, but he was poor in spelling, as many of his letters during the war reveal. By the end of his high school days, he possessed a standard, but not excellent, education.

In 1839, as a means of furthering his son's schooling, Grant's father applied to his congressman to secure an appointment at the U.S. Military Academy at West Point. Grant, who was a restless soul and took every opportunity to get away from home, consented to go, even though his father had not bothered to consult him regarding the opportunity.

"Devoted to Novels"

Upon his arrival at West Point, Grant discovered that he had been registered as Ulysses Simpson Grant. With diffidence that characterized him all his life, he never bothered to correct the error. Only five foot seven inches tall, the quiet, undistinguished cadet was often overlooked at the academy, doing only moderately well, as he later noted in his memoirs:

> I did not take hold of my studies with avidity, in fact I rarely ever read over a lesson the second time during my entire cadetship. . . . There is a fine library connected with the Academy from which cadets can get books to read in their quarters. I devoted more time to these, than to books relating to the course of studies. Much of the time, I am sorry to say, was devoted to novels, but not those of a trashy sort.[94]

On graduating in 1843, Grant was commissioned a second lieutenant of infantry, despite his talents with horses that would have served him well in the cavalry. Stationed near St. Louis, Missouri, he met and fell in love with Julia Dent, whom he married four years later after a stint in Louisiana and Texas during the Mexican War. The couple were very close, and Grant depended on his wife for support and happiness all his life. During the war, Julia was at his side at every possible opportunity.

After his marriage, Grant was transferred to Oregon Territory and later to a remote outpost in California. There, depressed and lonely, he began drinking heavily. In 1854 he resigned from the army and returned to Missouri to be closer to his family and try to make a living.

Grant enjoyed life as a civilian, but making enough money to support his wife and children proved difficult. He became a farmer and worked long days planting potatoes and building a house, "Hard-scrabble," on a piece of land owned by Julia's father. In 1856 he wrote his father, "Every day I like farming better and I do not doubt but that money is to be made at it." [95] Despite his optimism, low crop prices made farming a profitless enterprise. To feed his family in the winter, Grant peddled firewood in St. Louis and borrowed money from family and neighbors to keep the farm operative.

In 1858 the Grants abandoned farming and moved to St. Louis, where Grant tried to make a living as a bill collector. He was too quiet and unassertive to make a success of that, so in the summer of 1860 he and his family moved to Galena, Illinois. There Grant worked as a clerk in a harness shop his father now owned. His two younger brothers were making a success of the store, but Grant had no particular interest in shopkeeping. Nevertheless, he did his best to fit into Galena society, spending his evenings with Julia and the children in their small brick home, attending the Methodist church on Sunday, and actively recruiting volunteers when the government began calling for troops in the spring of 1861.

Call to War

When the war began, Grant offered his services to the army, but it was two months before the West Point graduate received a commission. Finally appointed a colonel, he set off in early summer at the head of the Twenty-first Illinois Regiment for Missouri. Grant was proud of his men, even though they were volunteers, not professional soldiers. He wrote "My men behaved admirably. . . . They can now go into camp after a day's march with as much promptness as veteran troops; they can strike their tents and be on the march with equal celerity [speed]." [96]

As they crossed into Missouri, Grant and his men had their first contact with the enemy. An encampment of Confederates lay in their path, and a run-in seemed inevitable. Grant was admittedly nervous, but when he and his men moved forward, they discovered that the enemy had fled. It was a revealing moment. He wrote:

> It occurred to me at once that Harris [the Confederate leader] had been as much afraid of me as I had been of him. This was a view . . . I had never taken before; but it was one I never forgot afterwards. From that event to the close of the war, I never experienced trepidation upon confronting an enemy. . . . I never forgot that he had as much reason to fear my forces as I had his. The lesson was valuable. [97]

Perfectly Trained

Although relatively inexperienced in the art of war in 1861, Ulysses Grant slowly but surely developed the skills he needed to lead the Union to victory. T. Harry Williams describes that learning process in Lincoln and His Generals.

"At the beginning of the war, Grant knew as much about the theory and history of war as the average West Point graduate and regular army officer, which was not very much. He did not, after the conflict started, study the higher art of war from books, but he studied it closely from the events he witnessed and experienced. At [Forts] Henry and Donelson, he saw the moral value of being on the offensive, and he learned at Shiloh the danger of neglecting the principle of precaution. In nearly all of his early operations, he demonstrated that he understood one of the most important of all strategic principles, that of making the destruction of the enemy army his primary objective. Grant absorbed some of his knowledge of war from other officers, and on many occasions used the brains of others, which is what a great general should do. As Sherman well expressed it, Grant possessed 'in an eminent degree that peculiar and high attribute of using various men to produce a common result. . . .' His brilliant victories at Vicksburg and Chattanooga were partly the result of his own developing strategic powers and partly of his ability to use the powers of his subordinates to accomplish his purpose. When he became general in chief, Grant was about as perfectly trained and formed for the post as any general could be."

Grant's confidence was further boosted by a promotion to brigadier general, which he received late that summer. It was a fairly routine step for regular army officers and former officers, but Grant was unused to such rewards and took the advance as a rare compliment.

Uncompromising Terms

While McClellan and the Army of the Potomac remained idle in the east, Grant found plenty of opportunities to thwart the enemy in the west. In September 1861, he learned that Confederate forces planned to advance on Paducah, Kentucky, a short distance from his headquarters. To block their move, he got to Paducah first and occupied the town without a shot being fired. In February 1862, he was part of an attack force that moved on Fort Henry, a Confederate stronghold on the Tennessee River. After taking the fort,

Grant's soldiers overtake the Confederates at Fort Donelson, forcing the unconditional surrender of the Rebels.

Grant marched his men a few miles east to Fort Donelson, "the gate to Nashville." [98] There his men lay siege to the fort. When the Confederate commander—a former friend of Grant's—asked for a truce so that they might discuss terms of surrender, Grant was resolute. "No terms except an unconditional and immediate surrender can be accepted." [99] The Confederates unhappily submitted, making Fort Donelson one of the first important Union victories of the war.

Grant's uncompromising words were soon repeated throughout the country by delighted Northerners, who were tired of generals who hesitated to push the enemy. They declared that Grant's initials—U.S.—stood for "Unconditional Surrender," and they adopted the general as their hero. Lincoln, who was pleased with Grant's unexpected determination and his capture of large stretches of Confederate-held territory in Tennessee, promoted him to major general.

Shiloh

Not every victory would be as easily won or as clear-cut as Fort Donelson. In early April, Grant was taken by surprise when Confederates attacked near Pittsburg Landing, Tennessee. He rallied his men, and the two sides clashed in a battle that centered around a small country church named Shiloh. By the end of the two-day conflict, there were about twenty-four thousand total casualties—

more than in the Revolutionary War, the War of 1812, and the Mexican War combined. Following the fight, Grant looked out over the bloody battleground with great sorrow. He wrote, "I saw an open field . . . so covered with dead that it would have been possible to walk across the clearing, in any direction, stepping on dead bodies, without a foot touching the ground." [100]

Despite his unpreparedness and his losses, Grant did not panic or retreat in the Battle of Shiloh. Neither side was credited with a decisive victory, but the North gained ground in Tennessee, and the general learned a valuable lesson. After Shiloh, he was always prepared to fight. Never again did he assume that the enemy would wait for him to attack.

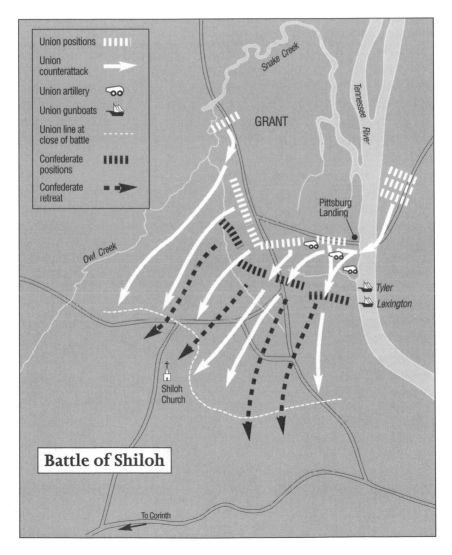

Battle of Shiloh

The Siege of Vicksburg

For a time, Grant's effectiveness was hampered by his superior, General Henry Halleck, who feared that this popular subordinate might try to usurp his authority and did what he could to shoulder Grant aside, even temporarily removing him from command. Grant was depressed by Halleck's maneuvering and considered resigning from the army, but a well-timed visit from his friend William Tecumseh Sherman changed his mind. "General Sherman happened to call on me as I was about starting and urged me so strongly not to think of going, that I concluded to remain." [101]

Halleck was promoted to general in chief in mid-1862 and moved to Washington. Shortly thereafter, Grant became head of the Army of the Tennessee. Back in command, he began making plans to capture the heavily fortified town of Vicksburg, Mississippi, which lay to the south, overlooking the Mississippi River. "A long line of high rugged irregular bluffs, clearly cut against the sky, crowned with cannon which peered ominously from embrasures to the right and left as far as the eye can see—that is Vicksburg," he wrote.[102] If the town could be captured, the South would be split and the Union would control the last railroad running east from the Mississippi River.

Union forces (foreground) rush to return enemy fire during the Battle of Shiloh, which resulted in twenty-four thousand casualties.

Grant's men lay siege to Vicksburg. The Southern town surrendered after a two-month bombardment.

In the fall of 1862, Grant began his first attempt to take Vicksburg. For months, however, he was thwarted in his approach by the swamps and bayous north of the town, as well as Confederate heavy artillery trained on the Mississippi. Finally in the spring of 1863, with the nation doubting his chance of success, he circled his troops in from the south and began shelling Vicksburg's fortifications.

When those proved too strong to penetrate, Grant determinedly turned to siege tactics. His artillery pounded Vicksburg for forty-eight days while Union boats shelled it from the river. Again, the nation speculated on his ability to take the town, especially when rumors of his heavy drinking reached their ears. Only Lincoln's support and protection kept him from being removed from command. "I rather like the man," the president said. "I think I'll try him a little longer." [103]

Lincoln's trust was repaid on July 4, 1863. After almost two months of siege, citizens of Vicksburg were desperate enough to concede defeat. Union soldiers celebrated the victory and the Fourth of July by publicly reading the Declaration of Independence and flying the American flag over the town. One of many jubilant Northerners, Captain Ira Miltmore, wrote his wife, "The backbone of the Rebellion is this day broken. The Confederacy is divided. . . . Vicksburg is ours. The Mississippi River is opened, and Gen. Grant is to be our next President." [104]

Although Grant was one of the most talented commanders of the war, he was also a human being with faults and weaknesses.

Many of those faults—poor business judgment and political naïveté—became all too apparent later in his life. During the war, the weakness that was most potentially harmful was drinking.

Both Grant's friends and his enemies were aware of this problem, which had begun early in his military career and often reoccurred when he was bored. His periods of intoxication did not seem to impair his ability to think and act quickly in battle, although his friends worried that they might. Friend and staff member John Rawlins tried unsuccessfully to convince Grant to give up liquor for the course of the war. "Had you not pledged me . . . that you would drink no more during the war, and kept that pledge during your recent campaign, you would not to-day have stood first in the world's history as a successful military commander," he reminded Grant, who had returned to the bottle during the long, frustrating siege of Vicksburg.[105]

An 1864 photograph captures Grant, now general in chief, at his camp in Virginia.

With rare restraint, newspaper reporters played down Grant's bouts of drinking, believing that the information would damage the general's reputation just when the country needed to trust its leaders. Rumors abounded, however, and throughout his lifetime, many of Grant's mistakes and oddities of behavior were attributed to his drinking.

General in Chief

Because of his success at Vicksburg and his growing popularity with Lincoln, in October 1863 Grant was assigned to head up all the armies in the West. In March 1864, after Congress had passed a bill reviving a rank previously held only by George Washington, Grant was promoted to lieutenant general and given command of the entire Union army. This force, now numbering 533,000 men, was the largest of its kind in the world.

It soon became apparent that Grant had both the wisdom and talent to be a high commander. Rather than isolate himself in

Washington, he chose mobile headquarters with the Army of the Potomac and capably directed the entire war effort from there. When General George Meade, head of the Army of the Potomac, offered to give up his command so that Grant could choose his own man for the job, Grant asked Meade to remain, impressed with a commander who would put the good of the country before his career. "This incident gave me even a more favorable opinion of Meade than did his great victory at Gettysburg the July before," he remarked.[106] The short-tempered Meade, who had assumed command of the Army of the Potomac just prior to the Battle of Gettysburg and had disappointed Lincoln by not pursuing Lee after the battle, benefited from Grant's almost continuous presence throughout the remainder of the war.

Grant lacked the charisma that made McClellan and Burnside so popular, but he was admired and respected by his troops, who trusted him implicitly. "There goes the old man," "Ulyss don't scare," and "Pretty hard nut for Johnny Reb to crack," they would say affectionately when Grant rode past.[107] "His soldiers do not salute him, they only watch him with a certain sort of familiar reverence. They observe him coming, and rising to their feet gather on each side of the way to see him pass," another observed.[108]

"Butcher Grant"

Grant also worked well with Lincoln, and together they formed an overall strategy for conducting the war. In a coordinated offensive against the South, the Armies of the Potomac and the James (under Meade and Butler) would move from the north and south against Lee and Richmond. "Wherever Lee goes, there you will go also," Grant told Meade.[109] General Sherman and his troops would advance into Georgia to capture Atlanta, while General Nathaniel Banks would head to Mobile. "Those not skinning can hold a leg," Lincoln noted approvingly.[110]

Even with a grand strategy, Grant knew that winning the war would not be easy. Robert E. Lee was a formidable opponent, and the Confederates were determined fighters. Beginning in May 1864, Union and Confederate armies clashed repeatedly, first in the Battle of the Wilderness, where Northern troops stumbled blindly through thick forests, impenetrable thickets, and bogs spotted with quicksand, and then died screaming in underbrush set afire in battle. "[Men were] piled upon each other in some places four layers deep, exhibiting every ghastly phase of mutilation," one Union soldier wrote thirty years later.[111]

Later that month, Grant and Lee faced off again in the Battle of Spotsylvania Court House, "the most terrible day I ever lived," according to another Union veteran.[112] Then came the Battle of Cold Harbor in June, where Union men were cut down by the thousands as they walked squarely into Confederate guns. Each confrontation produced heavy casualties on both sides; in one month, the Army of the Potomac lost fifty thousand men. With no definitive Union victories to offset the fatalities, the newspapers began calling the general "butcher Grant."

Grant himself felt the loss of so many men, and tried to spare their lives whenever he could. Nevertheless, he saw death as a necessary element of war, although his strategy was to ensure that more Confederates than Federals were killed. "The art of war is simple enough," he wrote. "Find out where your enemy is. Get at him as soon as you can. Strike at him as hard as you can and as often as you can, and keep moving on."[113] Such tenacity built his reputation even among his enemies. "Grant doesn't care a snap if men fall like the leaves fall, he fights to win, that chap does. He has the disagreeable habit of not retreating before irresistible veterans," wrote Southerner Mary Chesnut.[114]

General Grant relays orders amidst the confusion of the Battle of the Wilderness.

Siege of Petersburg

In June 1864 Grant decided that his frontal assaults on Lee were proving more bloody than productive, so he changed his strategy. In a quick and secret move, he directed Union troops to march south across the James River, then advance on the small town of Petersburg, Virginia, in an attempt to capture railroads that supplied Lee's troops.

Petersburg was strongly defended, however, and Lee's quick arrival on the scene made it stronger. Unable to take the city by assault, Grant once again turned to siege tactics. For nine months his heavy artillery pounded the city, while his troops and Lee's faced off, sniping at each other from behind entrenchments.

A Union soldier (foreground) stands beside a mortar used during the nine-month siege of Petersburg, Virginia.

"Nothing for excitement except that if you were picked off by sharpshooters. The feeling prevails that sooner or later this experience will befall us all," remarked Private John W. Haley.[115]

The wait was extended, but Grant was confident the city would eventually fall. He knew that the Confederate army was badly weakened by disease, losses on the battlefield, and lack of food and supplies. During the months of siege, he concentrated on weakening the enemy on other fronts—setting cavalryman Philip Sheridan to clear the Shenandoah Valley of Confederates, and supervising Sherman as he marched through Georgia and the Carolinas.

In the spring of 1865, the siege of Petersburg ended at last. On April 1, Union forces battled their way through Confederate defenses and drove the war-weary enemy out of town. Two days later, the Confederate capital of Richmond fell. Northern forces entered that city on the heels of the Confederate government, which had evacuated to Danville, one hundred twenty-five miles to the southwest.

Pushing Lee toward defeat in the final days of the war was a highly stressful period for Grant, who was also suffering from one of his rare "sick" headaches, which lasted several days. These headaches, according to George Meade, "cause him fearful pain such as almost overcomes his iron stoicism." [116]

Surrounded by their generals, Robert E. Lee (seated, left) and Ulysses S. Grant discuss the terms of the South's surrender in the parlor of Wilmer McLean, a resident of Appomattox Court House.

Lee did not make Grant's suffering easier. Outnumbered almost five to one and without hope of reinforcements, the Confederates doggedly retreated southwest from Richmond with portions of Grant's army in hot pursuit. Finally, after several desperate attempts to put off the inevitable, Lee sent a message to Grant on April 9, surrendering his troops. On hearing the news, Grant's terrible headache disappeared as if by magic.

The formal surrender of Lee's army to Grant took place that same day in a private home at the crossroads town of Appomattox Court House, Virginia. It was a momentous but oddly informal occasion, as historian William McFeely describes.

> Grant walked into the parlor and shook hands with Lee.
> . . . They talked about old times in the army in Mexico for so long that Lee had to remind Grant why they were there. Grant then took a pencil and paper and, with his usual directness, wrote that he would accept a surrender. . . . He ordered all equipment and supplies turned over to the Union army, except side arms, privately owned horses, and personal baggage. The men who surrendered, he added, would be allowed to go home.[117]

Except for formalities, the Civil War was over. At the end of the meeting, Lee returned to his men. Grant sent a message to Washington, announcing the victory. He also silenced Union guns, which were firing a victory salute. He later wrote, "The Confederates were now our prisoners, and we did not want to exult over their downfall."[118]

Eighteenth President

In the eyes of Union supporters, Grant had won the Civil War for the North, and, in 1866, Congress made him commanding general of the army with the rank of full general, a classification unused since the days of George Washington. Grant remained so popular in following years that Republicans enthusiastically nominated him for president in 1868. He won easily, promising "the greatest good for the greatest number."[119] His two terms in the White House were marked by scandal and corruption, however. During that time a small number of men—some of them high in the administration—enriched themselves at the expense of ordinary American citizens. Grant himself proved to be honest, but politically naive.

After his presidency, Grant and Julia took a two-year trip around the world, meeting heads of state from England to

Cruel Responsibility

Merciful to his enemies at the end of the war, Grant was also generous in his assessment of George McClellan, his predecessor as general in chief. Grant's generosity, described by John Y. Simon in Lincoln's Generals, *stemmed from his understanding of the enormous responsibilities shouldered by the first inexperienced commanders of the armies of the Union.*

"The test which was applied to him [McClellan] would be terrible to any man, being made a major-general at the beginning of the war. It has always seemed to me that the critics of McClellan do not consider this vast and cruel responsibility—the war, a new thing to all of us, the army new, everything to do from the outset, with a restless people and Congress. McClellan was a young man when this devolved upon him, and if he did not succeed, it was because the conditions of success were so trying. If McClellan had gone into the war as Sherman, Thomas, or Meade, had fought his way along and up, I have no reason to suppose that he would not have won as high a distinction as any of us. McClellan's main blunder was in allowing himself political sympathies, and in permitting himself to become the critic of the President, and in time his rival."

Japan, and peering at sights like typical tourists. They returned in time for Grant to be a leading contender in the Republican nominations for president in 1880, but he did not garner enough support to win.

In later years, Grant invested all his savings in a Wall Street investment firm that went bankrupt in 1884. Almost penniless, and dying of throat cancer, the former president decided to write a book about his war experiences. He tackled the project with the same resolution that helped him win the war, finishing it just days before his death. The two-volume work, published in 1885 by Grant's friend Samuel Clemens (Mark Twain), was popular enough to reestablish the family fortune.

Following the Civil War, Ulysses S. Grant served two terms as president of the United States.

Ulysses Grant died in Mount McGregor, New York, on July 23, 1885, at the age of sixty-three. He was temporarily buried in Central Park; then in 1897 his remains were placed in a newly built mausoleum—Grant's Tomb—on Riverside Drive, in Manhattan. His wife was interred beside him after her death in 1902. To the end of his life, Grant remained simple, patient, and determined, an ordinary man whose unexpected success in the war was as much a puzzle to himself as to others. In the words of his friend William T. Sherman, "Grant's whole character was a mystery even to himself—a combination of strength and weakness not paralleled by any of whom I have read in Ancient or Modern History." [120]

CHAPTER 6

Military Genius

By 1865, the outlook for the Union in the Civil War appeared brighter than ever before. Abraham Lincoln had been reelected as president. Ulysses Grant was hammering away at Robert E. Lee and his tattered Army of Northern Virginia. In Georgia, a tall, red-headed Ohioan and his men had taken Atlanta and were poised to slash their way through the Confederacy. "I can make Georgia howl!" William Tecumseh Sherman promised his friend Grant in late 1864.[121]

"At Home with Drum and Bugle"

The statement was typical of one of the most unconventional generals of the Union army. Sherman was born in Lancaster, Ohio, on February 8, 1820, the son of a state supreme court justice who died suddenly when the boy was nine. The judge's large family, which included ten children, split up to live with various friends and relatives. Young William was taken in by Ohio senator Thomas Ewing, who thereafter treated him as an adopted son.

After his father's death, the future Union general continued to attend Lancaster Academy, one of the best schools in the state. There he had excellent teachers and studied Latin, Greek, and French in addition to the traditional curriculum of mathematics and grammar. At Ewing's suggestion, the teenager also began preparing for entrance to the U.S. Military Academy at West Point, concentrating particularly on mathematics and French, two virtual prerequisites for admission.

In the spring of 1836, Sherman left the Ewing home and set out for West Point, stopping over at Washington along the way. There, to his delight, he was able to watch President Andrew Jackson pacing the gravel walkway on the north side of the White House. He also visited his uncles in New York City, where he met his cousin and her husband, who alienated him by treating him "as an untamed animal just caught in the far West."[122]

At the academy, the tall, red-haired cadet proved to be a bright student, good at chemistry, mathematics, drawing, and philosophy. Nevertheless, he was inclined to accumulate demerits for carelessness. "At the Academy I was not considered a good soldier, for at no time was I selected for any office, but remained a private throughout the whole four years," he wrote in his memoirs.[123] Despite these shortcomings, Sherman graduated sixth in his class of fifty-seven in 1840, and received an army commission as second lieutenant in the artillery, stationed in Florida.

Though Sherman had not been particularly happy at West Point, he remained in the military for more than ten years, serving in various posts and becoming "perfectly at home with drum and bugle."[124] In May 1850, he married Ellen Ewing, childhood friend and daughter of his foster father. In 1853, after a St. Louis banking firm asked him to be its representative in San Francisco, he resigned from the army to begin civilian life as a banker. California was in the grip of the gold rush, and the job looked like the beginning of a promising career for the thirty-three-year-old, who found life in a peacetime army monotonous and unrewarding.

William Tecumseh Sherman's military genius earned him the respect of even his enemies.

New Horizons

Sherman and his wife settled happily in San Francisco, and Sherman proved to be a capable banker. The bank collapsed, however, in the financial panic of 1857, leaving him without a job and without funds to pay off the company's investors. Conscientiously, he paid the debts himself, writing to Ellen who was visiting family in the East, "I am going to quit clean-handed—not a cent in my pocket. I know this is not modern banking, but better to be honest."[125]

Sherman next tried his hand at law, joining his brothers-in-law in their new practice in Leavenworth, Kansas, in 1858. When that proved unsatisfactory, he installed Ellen and the children with her parents and moved south to become the first superintendent of a newly established military academy, the Louisiana Seminary of Learning, later Louisiana State University. His intelligence and boundless energy made him well suited for his new responsibilities, which ranged from carpentry and bookkeeping to teaching and administration. The welfare of his students was his top priority, however, and they loved him as much as he cared for them. David Boyd, one of the professors at the academy observed, "the magnetism of the man riveted us all to him very closely, especially the cadets. . . . And if a cadet fell sick . . . he was at his bedside several times a day and at night, watching him closely."[126]

"Allegiance to the Constitution"

Despite his Ohio roots, Sherman shared many Southerners' racist attitudes about Negroes. Still, he believed strongly in the Union and so did not support secession. When war appeared inevitable, he reluctantly resigned his position at the school. "If Louisiana [withdraws] from the Federal Union, I hope to maintain my allegiance to the Constitution as long as a fragment of it survives, and my longer stay here would be wrong in every sense of the word," he wrote in his resignation on January 18, 1861.[127]

Reunited with his family, Sherman found work with a streetcar company in St. Louis. It was a good job, but he remained depressed over lost opportunities and the precarious fate of the nation. Many Northerners talked as if the coming struggle would be a short-lived skirmish, but Sherman foresaw an entirely different scenario. "This country will be drenched in blood. God knows how it will end," he said to a friend.[128] And to his wife's family, he wrote, "I think it is to be a long war—very long—much longer than any politician thinks."[129]

Unfit for Duty

Sherman did not immediately join the army at the outbreak of war, since he believed it would be run by politicians, whom he despised. Nevertheless he offered his services in May 1861, choosing to serve as a colonel in the regular army rather than a major general over volunteers. In the beginning, Sherman saw civilians as undisciplined, inferior soldiers. Soon, however, he grasped the fact that volunteers would be vital if the North was going to fight a prolonged war.

Sherman was promoted to brigadier general of volunteers shortly after the Union's first defeat at Bull Run (Manassas). He was assigned to the border state of Kentucky to hold it for the Union, and there, unhappy with his responsibilities and highly critical of the way the war was being conducted, he fretted, slept little, and became nervous and irritable.

Sherman's nervousness soon grew into a near-panicky fear of the enemy. He demanded sixty thousand reinforcements from the secretary of war to guard Kentucky's southern border, stating that two hundred thousand would be necessary if he were to make an offensive. Since his demands were unreasonable, highly emotional, and made in front of the press, newspaper stories soon appeared suggesting that he was irrational and unfit for duty. One newsman even hinted that he was insane.

Sherman was not having hallucinations or hearing voices, but he was close to a nervous breakdown, and in late 1861 he re-

Troubled Visionary

One of the few Americans to foresee the enormity of the Civil War, Sherman was at first not able to cope with his fears and the responsibilities he had been given. His reaction, and that of the press who witnessed it, is described by Michael Fellman in Lincoln's Generals, *edited by Gabor S. Boritt.*

"Despite his wishes, Sherman [was soon assigned a] command in Kentucky, a role he was mentally incapable of fulfilling. Sherman saw hidden enemies everywhere in Kentucky. He became convinced that such immense numbers of enemy troops were gathering in secret that he would need an army of 200,000 even to hold the state. This would have been twice the size of the Army of the Potomac. . . . Rather than keep such delusionary fears to himself, Sherman shared them both with newspapermen and with Secretary of War Simon Cameron, when Cameron visited him in Kentucky. Within a month of assuming command, Sherman had fallen into a deep, clinical depression, sleeping and eating little, smoking cigars, talking and probably drinking obsessively, pacing the corridors of

his hotel at night, alarming his staff with his loss of human contact and his increasingly compulsive habits. On November 9, 1861, Sherman was relieved of his command in disgrace, a fall from power soon broadcast by the newspapers across the nation, which all shouted on December 11 that Sherman had gone insane."

William Sherman buckled under the pressure of his responsibilities in the fall of 1861.

turned home to rest and recuperate. At the end of the year, he was reassigned to Kentucky, this time to serve under Ulysses S. Grant. Despite their different personalities, the two men became close friends. Sherman wrote:

> I am a damn sight smarter than Grant. I know a great deal more about war, military history, strategy, and grand tactics than he does. . . . But I tell you where he beats me, and where he beats the world. He don't care a damn for what the enemy does out of his sight, but it scares me like hell.[130]

Sherman was nervous and somewhat unsure of himself after his near breakdown, but Grant's friendship and trust helped build his confidence. In April 1862, Sherman played a significant role at the Battle of Shiloh, where he and his men stubbornly stood their ground after other Union troops had fled. That experience also boosted his self-confidence so that shortly thereafter, when he was promoted to major general, he took the new responsibility philosophically. He wrote to his wife, "I have worked hard to keep down, but somehow I am forced into prominence and might as well submit."[131]

Enlightened War

Sherman took part in several operations to open the Mississippi River in 1862 and the next year was part of the capture of Vicksburg under Grant. With Grant's promotion to commander in chief in March 1864, Sherman was given command of all the armies in the West. Confident that the war effort was now in good hands, he was as satisfied with Grant's announcement of a grand offensive as he was with his promotion. "That we are now all to act on a common plan, converging on a common centre, looks like enlightened war," he told Grant with satisfaction.[132]

Sherman's part in the offensive was an important one, which Grant entrusted only to his most capable general:

> You I propose to move against [Confederate general Joseph] Johnston's army, to break it up, and to get into the interior of the enemy's country as far as you can, inflicting all the damage you can against their war resources. I do not propose to lay down for you a plan of campaign, but simply to lay down the work it is desirable to have done, and leave you free to execute it in your own way.[133]

Sherman interpreted Grant's orders in terms of his own belief in total warfare—his armies would disrupt every aspect of Southern

Sherman (center), photographed here with his generals, took command of all of the armies in the west in March 1864.

life. Transportation and communication systems would be cut, factories and businesses destroyed, crops burned, and private property confiscated. He said, "We are not only fighting armies, but a hostile people, and must make old and young, rich and poor, feel the hard hand of war." [134]

To this end, he first reviewed the topography of Georgia and studied population and county records to be able to plan the best route for his army to follow. Taking Atlanta was a vital first step. The city was one of the few manufacturing centers of the South. It was an important railroad hub that linked the cities of the Confederacy with each other as well as with farming areas. It was also the gateway to the Atlantic states. Once that gate had been opened, the remainder of the Confederacy lay exposed to Union assault.

The Road to Atlanta

On May 5, 1864, Sherman and his army of one hundred thousand men set out from Chattanooga, Tennessee, on what was to become a year-long march. They traveled as light as possible. Each man carried five days' rations. Supplies were restricted to food and ammunition, and tents were left behind. Sherman wrote to the war office, "My entire headquarter's transportation is one wagon for myself, aides, officers, clerks, and orderlies. I think that is as low down as we can get." [135]

Despite his determination to travel light, Sherman tried to be prepared for every contingency on his march. He brought along several "dark wagons" in which engineers made copies of maps they drew while scouting the countryside ahead of the army. His men carried canvas pontoons, which could be thrown across rivers to create bridges. He maintained a crew to repair telegraph and railroad lines destroyed by Confederates. After use, the lines were again disabled. Rails in particular were pried loose, heated, and twisted beyond repair. His soldiers called them "Sherman's neckties" [136] and wrecked hundreds of miles of track in Georgia alone.

Sherman's creativity and his get-down-to-basics approach came as no surprise to his troops. Early in his command he had begun to ignore formalities such as dress reviews and maintained only a careless sort of discipline. This suited his men, since many were unpolished Midwesterners and volunteers from the hills who fought hard but paid no attention to manners or cleanliness. Others were teenage adventurers whom Sherman called "my little devils." [137] Sherman's casual camaraderie coupled with his skill as a leader endeared him to troops. They showed their affection not

As Sherman (on horseback) surveys the landscape during his long march to Georgia, his troops pry up railroad tracks to prevent them from being used by the Confederates.

only by his nicknames—Old Sherman and Uncle Billy—but by their loyalty and obedience to one who was temperamental and demanding, but never arrogant.

Terrible War

Throughout May and June, Sherman steadily pushed Joe Johnston's army across Georgia by flanking (moving around) the Confederates, attacking them from the side rather than head-on, and

---

The Complete Workman

William T. Sherman's colorful personality was matched by his unforgettable appearance, which grew more disheveled as time passed. In Sherman, *biographer B. H. Liddell Hart describes the general and his evening routine en route to Atlanta.*

"[He was] the complete 'workman,' indeed—with his black felt hat, unbraided and untasseled, pulled bulgingly over his high forehead and rather long, unkempt hair; the outline of his well-chiselled chin, small but strong, obscured yet emphasized by the short bristling fringe of his reddish whiskers and beard; his faded and threadbare coat unbuttoned to disclose a uniform vest buttoned only at the bottom and stained with the ash or nicotine of his endless chain of 'segars.'

His appearance by day was at least more presentable than by night when he was seen, poking at the camp-fire or prowling round a sleeping camp, with his bare feet in old slippers, his legs covered only by a pair of red flannel drawers, his tall, spare body wrapped in a travel-worn dressing gown. . . . As odd a figure as the hours he kept. For he was the most restless man and lightest sleeper in his army and not only shared with other great captains the power to maintain his activity on a slender allowance of sleep but had the habit of waking finally in the fourth hour of the morning. At this hour he liked to be up and about, thinking or listening—the 'best time,' as he said, 'to hear any movement at a distance.'"

A July 19, 1864, photograph of William Sherman shows the rugged general during his trek to Atlanta.

General Sherman leans on the breech of a cannon while consulting with his staff in the Union camp near Atlanta.

forcing them to fall back toward Atlanta. "Sherman'll never go to hell. He'll flank the devil and make heaven despite the guards," remarked one grim Confederate.[138] Sherman was at his best in such a situation, as one of his officers described:

> His eccentricities disappeared, his grasp of the situation was firm and clear, his judgment was cool and based upon sound military theory as well as quick practical judgment. . . . His mind seemed never so clear, his confidence never as strong, his spirit never so inspiring, and his temper never so amiable as in the crisis of some fierce struggle.[139]

By mid-July Atlanta was in sight, and Confederate president Jefferson Davis, who disliked Johnston, replaced him with General John B. Hood, a renowned fighter. Recognizing that he would not easily penetrate Atlanta's fortifications, Sherman decided to change his tactics. While shelling the town, he began shifting his troops around Atlanta, trying to encircle the city and capture its railroads, which acted as supply lines. With Hood cut off from reinforcements, he reasoned, the Confederates would soon be forced to surrender.

The Burning of Atlanta

The plan worked to a point. On September 1, 1864, Atlanta fell. Sherman captured the city, but Hood and his troops escaped. Nevertheless, the event was a Union triumph, and Sherman was the hero of the hour. Some Americans even suggested that he be promoted to lieutenant general, making him an equal—and perhaps a rival—of Grant. Sherman flatly refused the honor. "General Grant is a great general. I know him well. He stood by me when I was crazy, and I stood by him when he was drunk; and now, sir, we stand by each other always." [140]

Unwilling to leave troops behind to guard the city, and determined that it would not remain a symbol of Confederate resistance, Sherman ordered Atlanta destroyed. All industry—foundry, oil refinery, and freight warehouses—was demolished and set afire. Buildings such as theaters, stores, fire stations, and slave markets were burned. Sherman had directed that private homes be untouched, but uncontrolled fires spread to residential neighborhoods, driving families into the street. Major Henry Hitchcock, one of Sherman's aides, remembered:

> First bursts of smoke, dense, black volumes, then tongues of flame, then huge waves of fire roll up into the sky: Presently the skeletons of great warehouses stand out in relief against . . . sheets of roaring, blazing, furious flames . . . as one fire sinks, another rises . . . lurid, angry, dreadful to look upon. [141]

To the Sea

Leaving blackened Atlanta behind him, Sherman and his army set forth on the next step of their mission—cutting a sixty-mile wide swath of destruction across Georgia to the Atlantic coast. Planning to live off the land, Sherman's men carried little more than a blanket apiece, plus a tin cup, a rifle, and ammunition. Since communication could not be maintained with the North over such a distance, Sherman broke contact with his superiors. "I will not attempt to send couriers back, but trust to the Richmond [Confederate] papers to keep you well advised," he told Grant before he left. [142]

Living off the land meant that Sherman's army had to forage from Confederate homes and fields as it made its march. At first, the practice was disorganized, with inexperienced search parties sometimes competing with one another for available supplies.

Soon, however, each brigade was given responsibility for choosing twenty to fifty men to act as official foragers. The bummers, as they were called, daily rode out ahead of the army with their wagons in search of food and anything else that attracted their attention. A Union soldier described the plunder one such band brought to camp one evening:

> At the head of the procession . . . an ancient family carriage, drawn by a goat, a cow with a bell, and a jackass. Tied behind . . . a sheep and a calf, the vehicle loaded down with pumpkins, chickens, cabbages . . . squashes, a shoat [young pig], sorghum, a looking-glass, an Italian harp . . . a peacock, a rocking chair . . . a cradle, dried peaches, honey, a baby carriage, peach brandy and every other imaginable thing a lot of fool soldiers could take in their heads to bring away.[143]

During Sherman's march to the sea, Union bummers ransacked Southern homes and farms, confiscating food and supplies. Here, bummers pause in their efforts to determine whether approaching soldiers are Yankees or Rebels.

Bummers were not the only members of the army to take advantage of their military might. Union soldiers regularly plundered homes, chopped down trees, and stole family treasures. Some beat, raped, and murdered unprotected women and old people. "We had a gay old campaign," remembered one soldier in Sherman's army. "Destroyed all we could not eat . . . burned their cotton and gins, spilled the sorghum, burned and twisted their railroads and raised hell generally." [144]

Sherman did what he could to curb the violence, but he knew that such acts, although deplorable, would help bring the Confederacy to its knees. "War is the remedy our enemies have chosen and I say let us give them all they want," he declared. [145]

One of the Congregation

Confederates cursed Sherman and his troops, but former slaves saw them as a blessing. Throughout the march, thousands flocked

Separate and Unequal

Despite his admirable qualities, Sherman held many of the racist views common in America in the 1860s. His view on blacks and their ability to serve in the military is recounted by Michael Fellman in Lincoln's Generals, *edited by Gabor S. Boritt.*

"Of all the leading Union generals, Sherman was by far the most . . . overtly racist in his opposition [to Lincoln's policy of recruiting blacks into the army]. . . . In a letter to [his wife] Ellen he wrote, 'I would prefer to have this a white man's war and provide for the negroes after the time has passed. . . . With my opinion of negroes and my experience, yea prejudice, I cannot trust them yet. . . .'

In tandem with the prejudices of most of his soldiers, Sherman wanted to keep his troops free from the contamination they believed Negroes would bring. When Lorenzo Thomas [chief administrative officer] came west and addressed his men, informing them they would have to adjust to the presence of black troops, Sherman followed, telling his men . . . that he hoped that if the government did make use of black troops, 'they should be used for some side purpose & not be brigaded with white men.' 'I won't trust [negroes] to fight yet,' he wrote [his brother] John Sherman, adding that he did not oppose taking them from the enemy and finding other uses than combat for them. He was perfectly willing to use blacks as laborers and in 'pioneer brigades' to dig the trenches, build the forts, chop the wood and haul the water, all in aid to the . . . white soldiers."

Confederates despised General Sherman for his wanton destruction of Southern cities during his 1864 campaign. The ruins of Columbia, South Carolina, attest to the havoc wreaked by the Union general and his army.

to his camps, praising him as their savior, and begging him to protect them and take them North. "They gather around me in crowds and I can't find out if I'm Moses or Aaron but surely I am rated as one of the congregation," the general wrote.[146]

Grant encouraged Sherman to make good use of the many able-bodied blacks he encountered, recommending that the red-haired general "clean the country of Negroes and arm them." [147] Because of his racist views, Sherman largely ignored Grant's recommendation, although he did allow some young black men to enlist. He also regularly used former slaves as spies. One soldier said, "They were the only friends on whom we could rely for the sacred truth in Dixie." [148]

For the most part, however, Sherman had no patience with anyone or anything that impeded his progress, and soon became irritated by the blacks' continual presence. Nevertheless, he could do little to stop them, and vast numbers, particularly women and children, persistently followed the army in its march, relying on sympathetic Union soldiers to feed and protect them.

"A Christmas Gift"

Sherman disappeared into the heart of Georgia in mid-November 1864, and was not heard from again for over a month. In late December, however, he and his army reappeared on the Georgia

The victorious Union army parades through the nation's capital during the Grand Review. Throngs of crowds turned out to honor the soldiers who had defended the Union.

coast and triumphantly entered Savannah. "I beg to present to you as a Christmas gift the city of Savannah, with one hundred fifty heavy guns and plenty of ammunition, also about 25,000 bales of cotton," he telegraphed to Lincoln on December 24.[149] The announcement was welcomed by all Northerners, who not only delighted in Sherman's humor, but in the knowledge that they were winning the war at last.

Sherman allowed his men time to rest in Savannah, then began a relentless push north through the Carolinas. Despite the mud and winter weather, his armies accomplished ten miles a day, cutting down trees to make corduroy roads (logs laid crosswise) for their heavy artillery and destroying everything they left behind. Sherman's plans were so well laid that he and his men had to do relatively little fighting and thus did not rack up the huge losses suffered by Grant in many of his offensives.

Surrender

As planned, Sherman's march undermined the South's already weakened fighting spirit. "I made up my mind that there was no such army in existence since the day of Julius Caesar," admitted his adversary General Joseph E. Johnston, who was restored to his command about the time Sherman entered South Carolina.[150] After hearing of Sherman's onslaught, droves of Confederate soldiers deserted in order to return home and protect their families. Even Jefferson Davis remarked, "Sherman's campaign has produced bad effects on our people. Success against his future operations is needful to animate public confidence." [151]

Despite his brave words, even Davis knew that defeat for the Confederacy was only a matter of time. The fateful news that Lee had surrendered to Grant on April 9 percolated through the South just days before Sherman reached Raleigh, North Carolina. By the end of April, the red-haired Ohioan had accepted Joe Johnston's surrender near Durham, North Carolina.

The Union had won the war, and Sherman was, in the words of the *New York World*, "the idol of the day." [152] Generously he shared the credit with his army, saying to the crowds who thronged to him after the Grand Review, the Union army's victorious march through Washington, "I thank you for your kindness to me and the army I command," and later to the men themselves:

> How far the operations of this army contributed to the final overthrow of the Confederacy . . . must be judged by others, not by us; but you have done all that men could do . . . and we have a right to join in the universal joy that fills our land because the war is over. [153]

Respected and Admired

In the years after the war, Sherman remained in the military, a respected public figure who was repeatedly pressured to run for president. With unwavering firmness he turned down such suggestions. "I will not accept if nominated and will not serve if elected" was his most famous reply. [154] More to his taste was his

William Sherman continued to serve in the military after the Civil War; he finally retired in 1883.

appointment as commanding general of the army, dating from the time of his promotion to the rank of full general in 1869 until his retirement in 1883. In addition, he was a sought-after speaker at public dinners—often employing the theme "War is hell"—and served as an advocate for veterans who fell on hard times in postwar years.

As he grew older, Sherman spent many of his days at home, where he regularly put on an old pair of slippers and settled down with a cigar and a good book. In the evening, however, while his wife devoted herself to religious pursuits, he attended the opera, theaters, and balls, and was highly popular with the ladies. "I never saw a man so run after by womankind in my life," one observer remarked.[155]

On February 14, 1891, at the age of seventy-one, Sherman died of complications associated with asthma, a lifelong ailment. He was buried in St. Louis, Missouri. His old opponent, Joseph E. Johnston, served as honorary pallbearer at his funeral. Standing hatless in the winter weather, Johnston caught pneumonia, and less than five weeks later, he too was dead.

Respected by friends and enemies alike, William Tecumseh Sherman was a brilliant military strategist who believed in using all means at hand to save the Union, and just as strongly hoped for peaceful reconciliation with the South in the postwar years. His words, written to the leaders of Atlanta in the fall of 1864, reflect the unconventional creed of an extraordinary man.

> You cannot qualify war in harsher terms than I will. War is cruelty and you cannot refine it. . . . But, my dear sirs, when peace does come, you may call on me for any thing. Then will I share with you the last cracker, and watch with you to shield your homes and families against danger from every quarter.[156]

CHAPTER 7

Little Phil

It seemed inevitable that Philip Henry Sheridan should become a cavalry officer in the Civil War, if only because on horseback he appeared almost as tall as the men in his command. Standing, he was just five feet five inches, a wiry man with coarse black hair and a luxurious mustache.

Despite his short stature, Sheridan was, according to Ulysses Grant, "big enough for the purpose" when he went to battle during the final years of the Civil War.[157] Grant had good reason to trust in Sheridan. The young man's rise from store clerk to general was more meteoric than that of any other Union soldier in the war. Yet true to his roots, Sheridan never forgot to give credit to his men. "Put your faith in the common soldier and he will never let you down," he maintained.[158]

Philip Sheridan, the obscure store clerk who would rise to become a prestigious general.

"To Become a Soldier"

Philip Sheridan was born on or about March 6, 1831, of Irish immigrant parents. He claimed to have been born in Albany, New York, but his mother stated that he was born aboard ship bound for America from Ireland. The truth is not known.

Sheridan was raised in Somerset, Ohio, the third of six children, and attended a one-room schoolhouse where he learned the basics of English grammar and arithmetic. Like other boys, he got into trouble by skipping school, misbehaving in class, stealing apples, and fighting. Whenever he got the chance, he followed the town's one surviving Revolutionary War veteran around and eavesdropped at the local tavern, listening to tales told by Conestoga wagon drivers who stopped there for drinks.

No-Nonsense Fighter

Philip Sheridan was not only one of the youngest generals in the Civil War, he was also one of the smallest, weighing only one hundred fifteen pounds after one hard winter in Tennessee. What Sheridan lacked in size, however, he made up for in personality as author Roy Morris Jr. points out in Sheridan.

"Like his childhood hero Zachary Taylor, Sheridan was a gruff, informal, no-nonsense fighter who, while capable of a certain battlefield magnetism, had none of the elegant manners of a [Jeb] Stuart or a Lee. Instead, by way of compensation, he projected a nervous, tightly coiled energy that occasionally crossed into frontier-style violence. Once, when a southern railroad conductor treated him with less than adequate respect, Sheridan wordlessly interrupted a tête-à-tête with fellow general George H. Thomas, beat the offending party insensible, kicked him off his own train, and casually returned to his seat, picking up the thread of conversation with no explanation given and none required. The western farm boys and big-city easterners who served under him in his various commands may have called him 'Little Phil,' but they did so with affection, and they did so behind his back."

From his early days, Sheridan dreamed of the glory of battle. As a teen working in the town's general store, he took great interest in the Mexican War, and he became a local authority on the subject after studying newspaper accounts of the fighting. "The stirring events of the times so much impressed and absorbed me that my sole wish was to become a soldier, and my highest aspirations to go to West Point as a cadet." [159] For the time being he had to be content with clerking, and his willingness to please helped him quickly advance from stockboy to bookkeeper.

In 1848 Sheridan's wish to attend West Point came true. Nominated by his district congressman, he arrived at the U.S. Military Academy with high hopes and a fierce determination to succeed. The task was harder than he had anticipated. He was short, awkward, quarrelsome, and poorly educated, all qualities that worked against success at the school. He studied hard to make up for his academic shortcomings, but it was his fiery temper that almost ended his career prematurely. He got into a fist fight with a superior, and was suspended from West Point for a year. Angrily, he returned to Somerset and the general store, complaining of his "very unfair punishment." [160]

Sheridan returned to the academy unrepentant and just managed to graduate with the class of 1853, having earned a dangerously high number of demerits for infractions such as drinking, smoking, gambling, and smuggling food into his room. Because of his low standing in class, he was assigned to an infantry regiment stationed at Fort Duncan, a remote post in southwestern Texas.

The Way Up

By 1861, Sheridan had served at various posts throughout the West and spent his time skirmishing with Indians and impressing his superiors with his energy and resourcefulness. As the war began, numerous officers resigned from the army to join the Confederacy, leaving openings in the ranks that had to be filled. In March, Sheridan was promoted to first lieutenant, then abruptly raised to the rank of captain two months later. He remarked to a friend that, if things continued as they were, "perhaps I may . . . earn a major's commission."[161]

Because of his experience as a store clerk, Sheridan served for a time in Missouri as chief quartermaster—the officer in charge of purchasing and distributing food, clothes, and other supplies. By the spring of 1862, he had done nothing more heroic than forcing unwilling Missouri farmers to reveal hidden stashes of livestock and corn, which he needed to feed the army. After news of the Battle of Shiloh reached him, he requested and was granted a transfer to a fighting unit in Tennessee. His reputation as an efficient clerk and problem solver followed him, however, and he was again put to work securing and transporting supplies rather than pursuing Confederates.

"Worth His Weight in Gold"

Unexpectedly, on May 27, Sheridan received a telegram appointing him colonel of the Second Regiment Michigan Cavalry, stationed in northern Mississippi. Sheridan had never served with a cavalry unit before, but like most men of the day he knew how to ride, and he had plenty of self-confidence. He quickly fit in with his new regiment, personally seeing to their physical needs in the midst of his other military duties. "Men who march, scout, and fight . . . must have the best bodily sustenance, and every comfort that can be provided," he observed.[162]

Fortune again smiled on Sheridan in July, when some of his raiders came across a number of letters left behind by fleeing Rebels. The letters seemed to indicate that the Confederates intended to attack the Union forces of General Don Carlos Buell,

Union soldiers relax in their camp along the Tennessee River in Chattanooga, near where General Sheridan and his troops routed the Confederates during the Battle of Chattanooga.

headed for Chattanooga, Tennessee. Sheridan promptly forwarded the letters to his superiors, who were impressed by his actions. They telegraphed to Washington: "Brigadiers scarce. Good ones scarcer. . . . The undersigned respectfully beg that you will obtain the promotion of Sheridan. He is worth his weight in gold." [163]

General Sheridan

Sheridan received his promotion to brigadier general of volunteers in September 1862. In late December and early January he led a division in the Battle of Stones River (Murfreesboro), winning a reputation there as a "perfect tornado in battle," not only for his energy but for the profanity that colored his every utterance. General William Rosecrans, Sheridan's commanding officer at Stones River, remembered, "He was pouring such a volume of oaths [at his men] as made my blood curdle." [164]

A year later, Sheridan was part of the Union defeat at the Battle of Chickamauga. In November he helped recover that loss when, without waiting for orders, he and his men made a dramatic and unexpected charge up Confederate-held Missionary Ridge in the Battle of Chattanooga, sending the enemy scurrying down the other side. Sheridan captured numerous Confederate prisoners, artillery, and small arms in the battle; his actions won him praise from Grant, who was then commanding officer of the Army of the West.

Sheridan spent the weeks after the Battle of Chattanooga working to keep his men fed and sheltered in the chill Tennessee countryside. With his experience as a quartermaster, he was often able to obtain supplies when others could not. His men appreciated this dedication, calling him affectionately "Little Phil." Their leader was vain, volatile, and high strung, and he sometimes shifted blame to others' shoulders, but he was also brave and cool-headed in battle. It was not unusual for his men to see him at the head of a charge, unlike some leaders who remained safely in the rear. His men's trust translated to obedience, even during difficult times. As one observer recounted, during an engagement when his exhausted men were told to hold their ground at all costs, "the morale of the corps was so good and their confidence in Sheridan so great that when the order . . . was repeated, they never dreamed of leaving the spot." [165]

Cavalry Command

In April 1864, Sheridan received a call to Washington. Grant, now general in chief, was dissatisfied with the accomplishments of the cavalry of the Army of the Potomac. The dashing deeds of the Confederate cavalry under General J. E. B. Stuart were becoming legendary, while the Union cavalry had been used primarily to protect supply trains, serve as messengers,

Despite his egotism and volatile nature, Sheridan displayed extreme courage in battle and dedication to his troops.

and ride guard around the edges of the encamped army. Grant, who remembered Sheridan from the Battle of Chattanooga, assigned him the task of converting the cavalry into a strike force.

The officers and men of Sheridan's new command, one of whom was fiery young George Armstrong Custer, did not greet his coming with enthusiasm. First, the little general's appearance was against him. Abraham Lincoln described him as "a brown, chunky little chap, with a long body, short legs, . . . and such long arms that if his ankles itch he can scratch them without stooping." [166]

Next, he had been an infantry commander (most of his men knew nothing of his prior cavalry experience), and humble "foot-sloggers" were scorned by the cavalry.[167] Finally, Sheridan had served in the West, and Easterners were prejudiced against a man who had not shared their misery in such epic battles as Antietam, Fredericksburg, and Gettysburg.

Sheridan soon won them over, however, by his straightforward, businesslike approach to war, and by his habit of treating everyone fairly and equally. "He would as soon borrow a light from the pipe of an enlisted man as from the cigar of an officer," one soldier remarked. Sheridan also retained the staff of the former commander, one of whom observed, "[He] had no favorites but the men who best carried out his orders." [168]

Wily Rebel general J. E. B. Stuart (pictured) and his cavalry battled Sheridan and his Yankees at Yellow Tavern, Virginia; Stuart's death during the engagement rocked Confederate morale.

"Let Him Do It"

In his first month with the cavalry, Sheridan spent much of his time refitting it for service, since troops and their mounts had been overworked, underfed, and inadequately sheltered. Sheridan set about improving conditions and requesting additional horses. At the same time, he suggested to his superior, General George Meade, that scattered regiments of cavalry be consolidated and used in battle against Confederate cavalry. Meade disliked the idea and refused.

In May 1864 Sheridan had his first chance to prove the value of a top-notch cavalry. When Grant and Meade marched the Army of the Potomac into the Wilderness in Virginia, Sheridan was incensed to discover that he and his men had once again been assigned to guard supply trains rather than be a part of the offensive. As troops moved toward Spotsylvania, Sheridan confronted Meade, insisting that he could "thrash hell out of Stuart any day," if allowed to do so.[169]

When Meade reported his words to Grant, Grant quietly replied, "Well, [Sheridan] generally knows what he's talking about. Let him start right out and do it." [170] In the days that followed, Sheridan's ten thousand cavalrymen chased Stuart's three

Sheridan (far left) poses with his officers, including fearless George Armstrong Custer (far right).

thousand across the countryside. The two finally clashed at the hamlet of Yellow Tavern, Virginia, on May 11, 1864, where the Confederates were roundly defeated and Stuart was killed. His death was a blow to the Confederacy and did much to shake Southern morale.

The Army of the Shenandoah

Sheridan had finally proved that he and his cavalry were a true combat force. In July 1864 Ulysses Grant gave the cavalryman an assignment that, if successful, would go far toward bringing the war to a close.

For years the North had been all too aware of Rebel action in the Shenandoah Valley, a fertile strip of farmland controlled by the Confederates that lay just west of the nation's capital. The valley was known as "the back door on Washington," since it was easy for Rebel forces to threaten Washington from their vantage point there. The most recent threat consisted of General Jubal A. Early and his fifteen thousand Confederate troops, whose presence not only lowered Northern morale, but posed a potential threat to nearby Pennsylvania and Maryland.

Early was not the only enemy in the Shenandoah Valley. Union forces there were continually attacked by Confederate guerrilla bands known as irregulars. These daring men—soldiers and valley inhabitants—always seemed to be where they were least wanted.

They sniped at Union work parties, lobbed shells into Union camps, derailed trains, and in general kept Union soldiers nervous and on edge.

To drive Early and the irregulars out of the valley, Grant put Sheridan in charge of the newly formed Army of the Shenandoah. "I want Sheridan put in command of all the troops in the field, with instructions to put himself south of the enemy and follow him to the death. Wherever the enemy goes, let our troops go also," he explained to Lincoln.[171]

The Army of the Shenandoah was to be as ruthless as it was resolute. As it pushed through the valley, it was to destroy rail lines, communications, animals, and crops. Sheridan and his men were to live off the land. "Take all provisions, forage, and stock wanted for

A photograph taken in late 1864 depicts General Sheridan at ease in his camp during the Shenandoah Valley campaign.

the use of your command. Such as cannot be consumed, destroy," Grant commanded.[172] He reasoned logically that when there was nothing on which an army could live, Jubal Early and the irregulars would be irreparably crippled.

"War Is a Punishment"

Sheridan, who had never been given such an extensive assignment before, began his task in the Shenandoah Valley with uncharacteristic caution. He studied its makeup, pinpointing its roads, streams, mountains, and population centers. He carefully determined the strength of the enemy, since there was a possibility that Lee might send reinforcements when he understood Sheridan's intentions. Such careful preparations took time, and soon Secretary of War Stanton and other Washington officials questioned whether Sheridan was the right man for the job. He was very young—only thirty-three—and relatively inexperienced. Was he, like others before him, too hesitant to fight?

Sheridan soon allayed their fears by proving himself an able fighter. He did not win every battle, but when his army clashed with Confederates on September 19 at the town of Winchester, Sheridan emerged victorious. A message to Grant from Sheridan's chief of staff stated, "We have just sent [the Rebels] whirling through Winchester and we are after them tomorrow." [173] The good news was quickly passed on and the phrase, "whirling through Winchester" was jubilantly repeated throughout the North.

Sheridan, however, was not satisfied with his victory at Winchester. In November he ordered a division of his men to "consume and destroy all forage and subsistence, burn all barns and mills . . . and drive off all stock in the region." [174] Everything in the valley other than private homes was burned. "As war is a punishment, if we can, by reducing its advocates to poverty, end it quicker, we are on the side of humanity," Sheridan explained.[175]

The Burning

Like the army of William Tecumseh Sherman in Georgia and the Carolinas, Sheridan and his cavalrymen undermined the Confederacy by destroying the Shenandoah Valley in late 1864. Roy Morris Jr. describes the devastation in his biography, Sheridan.

"Dayton was merely one in a series of Shenandoah Valley towns fired that autumn by Federals in a deliberate campaign of looting and arson memorialized by its victims as 'the Burning.' While Union infantry and artillery started northward from Harrisonburg along the Valley Pike on October 6, the cavalry fanned out in a twenty-mile arc. . . . By the time they reached Woodstock, forty miles away, Sheridan's horsemen had burned more than two thousand barns and seventy grain mills, driven off four thousand head of cattle, and slaughtered three thousand sheep. . . .

Day after day the blue column moved northward, leaving in its wake a heavy pall of smoke clearly visible to the anguished Confederates trailing behind. The sheer remorselessness of the Yankees' deeds staggered soldier and civilian alike. . . . Occasionally a farmer tried fighting back, one man against many, but most did nothing except watch disconsolately as the backbreaking work of a lifetime flamed into ashes in a matter of seconds. Sheridan, who considered war a just punishment to be visited on anyone foolish enough to support it, rode in the vanguard of his devastating army, his feet propped up in a two-seater wagon, jauntily waving a cigar at his troops."

Route to Victory

"The Burning," as it was called, raised long-lasting bitterness among residents of the Shenandoah Valley, but slowed the activities of Confederate irregulars. Early's men remained unbeaten, however, and on October 19, 1864, they staged a surprise dawn attack that almost routed Sheridan's army.

The Union general had just returned from a war conference in Washington and had spent the night in Winchester when he awoke to the sounds of heavy cannon fire coming from the direction of Cedar Creek, some twelve miles away. Riding to investigate, he came face to face with hundreds of fleeing Federals. In the words of one of his officers, it was "a panic-stricken army—hundreds of slightly wounded men, throngs of others unhurt but utterly demoralized, and baggage-wagons by the score, all pressing to the rear in hopeless confusion." [176]

With no thought of retreat, Sheridan pushed his way to the front lines, cursing, shouting, rallying his men as he went. "Come on back! Face the other way. We're going to lick those fellows out of their boots!" he cried.[177] Encouraged by the return of their confident commander, most of the men did indeed turn around. "Now we all burned to attack the enemy, to drive him back, to retrieve our honor," one staff officer wrote.[178]

A valiant General Sheridan (center) rallies his cavalry during the Battle of Cedar Creek. Sheridan's confidence transformed the near retreat into a Union victory.

By evening, the episode had turned into a Union victory. Receiving word of it in Petersburg, Grant telegraphed to the president. "Turning what bid fair to be a disaster into a glorious victory, stamps Sheridan what I have always thought him—one of the ablest of generals," he said.[179]

A Humbug

Despite Sheridan's growing reputation as a Union hero, some of his colleagues and fellow officers had a different opinion. They saw the general as a blusterer and a braggart, a man who took credit for the accomplishments of others. In reality, they insisted, he had little genius for warfare at all.

General George Crook, who had attended West Point with Sheridan and fought with him in the Civil War, claimed that shortly after the Union victory at Cedar Creek,

Although Philip Sheridan was considered a hero by some civilians, many of his colleagues perceived him to be nothing but a phony braggart.

Sheridan had admitted that the Union panic and its subsequent victory would have occurred with or without his being there. Major General John M. Palmer, who had served with Sheridan early in his career, wrote in 1867:

> I know "Phil" well. . . . Have made two campaigns and have shared two great battles with him. . . . Stones River and Chickamauga. In both he was whipped out of his boots, and in both he gained more reputation by his pretense than by his acts. He was then, and still, is, a humbug.[180]

Despite such controversy over Sheridan's talents, the fact remained that Jubal Early's army was finally beaten and the back door on Washington closed. Sheridan received the thanks of Congress and was made a major general in the regular army. He would next go on to help Grant and Sherman wrap up the war.

Five Forks and Appomattox

Sheridan and his men left the Shenandoah Valley in February 1865. Grant had instructed them to head for North Carolina, since Sherman needed reinforcements there.

The orders were a disappointment to Sheridan, who sensed that the war was coming to a close and wanted to be with Grant—in the center of action—during its final days. He had been in the habit of reinterpreting or disregarding Grant's instructions when they displeased him, so now he headed for Grant's headquarters at Petersburg instead of supporting Sherman. As in the Shenandoah Valley, he and his men left a trail of devastation behind them as they crossed the state of Virginia.

When the cavalryman arrived in Petersburg, Grant, who was surprisingly tolerant of Sheridan's insubordination, allowed him to remain. Thus, Sheridan was in the thick of the action when Grant engaged Robert E. Lee's army at the Battle at Five Forks on April 1, 1865. There, Sheridan and his men did their part by defeating General George E. Pickett and taking prisoner more than five thousand men, many of whom sensed that the Confederacy was dying and surrendered without a fight. Author Clarence Edward Macartney writes,

> Sheridan was the very incarnation of battle. During a critical moment he seized his crimson and white battle flag and, waving it above his head, rode up and down in front of the line, shouting encouragement to his men, swearing, praying, entreating, and shaking his fist.[181]

When Richmond fell on April 3, Sheridan was almost too busy harassing Lee's army to notice. On April 6 at Saylor's Creek, he and his men cut off and captured seven thousand Confederates; the day after they were riding hard to cut off Lee's line of retreat to the south. The little general was readying for another attack on the Confederates early on April 9 when a messenger gave him the news. "Lee has surrendered; do not charge; the white flag is up."

Sheridan reined in his horse and held up his clenched fist. "I've got 'em like that!" he shouted jubilantly.[182]

It was a momentous occasion. After conferring with Confederate delegates under a flag of truce, Sheridan sent a messenger to bring Grant to the front. A meeting between Lee and Grant was set up for that afternoon at the crossroads town of Appomattox Court House. Sheridan made sure that he was one of the few to be there as the two commanding generals worked out the details of the surrender.

Business in the West

Sheridan was not part of the Grand Review, the victorious march of the Union army through Washington, which took place immediately after the war's end. No matter how much the little general argued, the normally tolerant Grant insisted that his subordinate was needed in the South "to restore Texas, and that part of Louisiana held by the enemy, to the Union in the shortest practicable time." [183] Sheridan was soon involved in Mexican border politics as well as in Reconstruction, the process of reestablishing Southern states as part of the Union.

Transferred to military duty in the West in mid-1867, Sheridan received the news of his promotion to the rank of lieutenant general on March 6, 1869, his thirty-eighth birthday. He spent much of the next fifteen years fighting the Apache, Sioux, Cheyenne, and other Native American tribes, pausing in 1875 to get married. His bride, captivating Irene Rucker, was only half the lifelong bachelor's age, but friends felt the two made an ideal couple.

Irene's influence did much to improve Sheridan's rough manners,

After the war Philip Sheridan was transferred to the western frontier, where he battled Native Americans and protected pioneers.

but he remained a fighter throughout his life. Always outspoken, Sheridan's most famous statement, "The only good Indians I ever saw were dead," revealed a deplorable but commonly held prejudice of the times.[184] Sheridan, however, did more than his share to ensure that pioneers were safe from attack while crossing the plains.

In 1884, upon William Tecumseh Sherman's retirement from the military, Sheridan became commanding general of the U.S. Army. Now overweight and short of breath, he lived and worked in the capital until he suffered a heart attack in early 1888. The once fiery little general died on August 5 of that year and was buried in Arlington National Cemetery. He was only fifty-seven years old. Despite her youth, Irene never remarried, declaring, "I would rather be the widow of Phil Sheridan than the wife of any man living." [185]

Mourned by the nation, Sheridan was remembered as a great general and a staunch defender of the Union. Just prior to his death, Congress voted to award him the rank of full general, an honor held only by Sherman and Grant. In the words of the latter, "I believe General Sheridan has no superior as a general, either living or dead, and perhaps not an equal." [186]

Unsung Heroes

The Civil War brought about changes in the United States that were numerous, complex, and far-reaching. The Confederacy was defeated, and the Union secured, proof to the world that the United States of America was not just a collection of states, but a single, unified nation. Slavery was abolished, although it would be years before blacks were granted equality. The traditional Southern way of life all but disappeared, to be replaced by a heritage of bitterness and division that would plague the nation for generations to come.

A veteran of the Civil War proudly holds the tattered remains of the battle flag carried by the Eighth Pennsylvania Volunteers.

Personal Victories

To the generals—along with every soldier who lived through the conflict—the war's end was a personal victory. They had survived cold, hunger, Minie balls, and bayonet charges. Many had been hampered in their efforts by interfering politicians and backstabbing associates. All had confronted fear and cheated death. From the youngest—Galusha Pennypacker, who was not old enough to vote in 1864—to the oldest—John E. Wool, born three years after the end of the Revolutionary War—each man had sacrificed a portion of himself for the greater good of the country. The rest of their days were colored by the momentous ordeal through which they had come.

In the vast catalog of those who served, many rose to high positions in the war, but did little to deserve their titles. Some who fought most valiantly have been all but forgotten. One of the latter was General Joseph Jackson Bartlett, who was repeatedly commended by his superiors for exceptional service with the Army of

A Permanent Possession

The Civil War not only changed the lives of the men who fought in it, it has had an effect on the nation that remains even to the present as Pulitzer Prize–winner Bruce Catton notes in his history, This Hallowed Ground.

"[The Civil War] had laid an infinity of loss and grief on the land; it had created a shadowed purple twilight streaked with undying fire which would live on, deep in the mind and heart of the nation, as long as any memory of the past retained meaning. Whatever the American people might hereafter do would in one way or another take form and color from this experience. Under every dream and under every doubt there would be the tragic knowledge bought by this war, the awareness that triumph and disaster are the two aspects of something lying beyond victory, the remembrance of heartbreak and suffering, and the moment of vision bought by people who had bargained for no vision but simply wanted to live at peace. A new dimension had been added to the national existence, and the exploration of it would take many generations. The Civil War, with its lights and its shadows, its unendurable pathos and its charred and stained splendor, would be the American people's permanent possession."

the Potomac in every battle (except Second Manassas) from Manassas to Appomattox. Another in the list of unsung heroes is General Winfield S. Hancock, who, according to Grant, "never . . . committed in battle a blunder," [187] and whose skill helped the Union at Antietam, Gettysburg, the Wilderness, Spotsylvania, Petersburg, and other locales.

General Alfred H. Terry, one of the few generals in the regular army who did not attend West Point, won his men's confidence "by his coolness in action and by his clearness of perception." [188] Benjamin F. Davis, who was not a general but should have been, was the only officer from the Deep South who remained loyal to and fought for the Union during the war.

From the youngest to the oldest, whether remembered or forgotten, all Union generals had a part to play in this unique period of U.S. history. Their individual contributions may have been lost in time, but the great national good they accomplished will never fade. In the words of General Joshua Lawrence Chamberlain, one of the all-but-forgotten, "What we had lost and what we had won had passed into the nation's peace; our service into her mastery, our worth into her well-being, our life into her life." [189]

NOTES

Introduction: An Untested Company

1. Bruce Catton, *This Hallowed Ground*. New York: Doubleday, 1956, p. 36.

2. Quoted in Ken Burns, *The Civil War* (video recording). Beverly Hills, CA: Pacific Arts Video, 1990, episode 2.

3. Quoted in Burns, *The Civil War*, episode 9.

Chapter 1: A Personal War

4. Burns, *The Civil War*, episode 1.

5. Quoted in Burns, *The Civil War*, episode 1.

6. Quoted in Burns, *The Civil War*, episode 1.

7. Quoted in Catton, *This Hallowed Ground*, p. 3.

8. Quoted in Burns, *The Civil War*, episode 1.

9. Quoted in Burns, *The Civil War*, episode 2.

10. Quoted in Burns, *The Civil War*, episode 1.

11. Quoted in Burns, *The Civil War*, episode 4.

12. Catton, *This Hallowed Ground*, p. 329.

13. Quoted in Burns, *The Civil War*, episode 7.

14. George B. McClellan, *McClellan's Own Story*. New York: Charles L. Webster, 1887, p. 31.

Chapter 2: Young Napoleon

15. Quoted in Stephen W. Sears, *George B. McClellan, The Young Napoleon*. New York: Ticknor & Fields, 1988, p. 4.

16. Quoted in Sears, *George B. McClellan*, p. 3.

17. Quoted in Sears, *George B. McClellan*, p. 4.

18. Quoted in Sears, *George B. McClellan*, p. 10.

19. Quoted in Sears, *George B. McClellan*, p. 30.

20. Quoted in Sears, *George B. McClellan*, p. 66.

21. Quoted in Sears, *George B. McClellan*, p. 62.

22. Quoted in Sears, *George B. McClellan*, p. 66.

23. Quoted in Sears, *George B. McClellan*, p. 70.

24. Quoted in Sears, *George B. McClellan*, p. 93.

25. T. Harry Williams, *McClellan, Sherman and Grant*. Rutgers, NJ: Rutgers University Press, 1962, p. 17.

26. McClellan, *McClellan's Own Story*, p. 82.

27. T. Harry Williams, *Lincoln and His Generals*. New York: Knopf, 1952, p. 29.

28. Quoted in Sears, *George B. McClellan*, p. 101.

29. McClellan, *McClellan's Own Story*, p. 86.

30. Sears, *George B. McClellan*, p. 104.

31. McClellan, *McClellan's Own Story*, p. 225.

32. McClellan, *McClellan's Own Story*, pp. 424–25.

33. McClellan, *McClellan's Own Story*, p. 531.

34. McClellan, *McClellan's Own Story*, p. 567.

35. Quoted in Sears, *George B. McClellan*, p. 265.

36. Quoted in Sears, *George B. McClellan*, p. 267.

37. Quoted in Sears, *George B. McClellan*, p. 270.

38. Quoted in Sears, *George B. McClellan*, pp. 319–20.

39. McClellan, *McClellan's Own Story*, p. 614.

40. Quoted in Sears, *George B. McClellan*, p. 338.

41. Quoted in Sears, *George B. McClellan*, p. 227.

42. Quoted in Sears, *George B. McClellan*, p. 367.

43. Quoted in Sears, *George B. McClellan*, pp. 367–68.

44. Quoted in Sears, *George B. McClellan*, p. 386.

45. Quoted in Sears, *George B. McClellan*, p. 388.

46. Quoted in Sears, *George B. McClellan*, p. 401.

Chapter 3: Reluctant Commander

47. William Marvel, *Burnside*. Chapel Hill: University of North Carolina Press, 1991, p. 35.

48. Quoted in Clarence Edward Macartney, *Grant and His Generals*. New York: McBride, 1953, p. 246.

49. Marvel, *Burnside*, p. 39.

50. Quoted in McClellan, *McClellan's Own Story*, pp. 244–45.

51. Marvel, *Burnside*, p. 95.

52. Marvel, *Burnside*, pp. 99–100.

53. Marvel, *Burnside*, p. 163.

54. Quoted in Marvel, *Burnside*, p. 162.

55. Catton, *This Hallowed Ground*, p. 187.

56. Quoted in Burns, *The Civil War*, episode 4.

57. Catton, *This Hallowed Ground*, p. 189.

58. Quoted in Williams, *Lincoln and His Generals*, p. 200.

59. Marvel, *Burnside*, p. 200.

60. Quoted in Marvel, *Burnside*, p. 200.

61. Quoted in Macartney, *Grant and His Generals*, p. 248.

62. Quoted in Macartney, *Grant and His Generals*, pp. 248–49.

63. Quoted in Macartney, *Grant and His Generals*, pp. 257–58.

64. Marvel, *Burnside*, p. 407.

65. Quoted in Burns, *The Civil War*, episode 7.

66. Quoted in Marvel, *Burnside*, p. 417.

67. Quoted in Marvel, *Burnside*, p. 425.

Chapter 4: The Beast

68. Robert S. Holzman, *Stormy Ben Butler*. New York: Macmillan, 1954, p. 7.

69. Quoted in Holzman, *Stormy Ben Butler*, p. 18.

70. Quoted in Holzman, *Stormy Ben Butler*, p. 14.

71. Quoted in Williams, *Lincoln and His Generals*, p. 214.

72. Quoted in Holzman, *Stormy Ben Butler*, p. 35.

73. Quoted in Dick Nolan, *Benjamin Franklin Butler, the Damnedest Yankee*. Novato, CA: Presidio Press, 1991, pp. 101–102.

74. Quoted in Holzman, *Stormy Ben Butler*, p. 66.

75. Quoted in Holzman, *Stormy Ben Butler*, p. 68.

76. Quoted in Burns, *The Civil War*, episode 5.

77. Holzman, *Stormy Ben Butler*, p. 84.

78. Quoted in Nolan, *Benjamin Franklin Butler*, p. 177.

79. Quoted in Nolan, *Benjamin Franklin Butler*, p. 179.

80. Quoted in Holzman, *Stormy Ben Butler*, p. 86.

81. Quoted in Nolan, *Benjamin Franklin Butler*, p. 175.

82. Quoted in Holzman, *Stormy Ben Butler*, p. 83.

83. Quoted in Holzman, *Stormy Ben Butler*, p. 93.

84. Quoted in Holzman, *Stormy Ben Butler*, pp. 92–93.

85. Quoted in Holzman, *Stormy Ben Butler*, p. 102.

86. Quoted in Holzman, *Stormy Ben Butler*, pp. 104–105.

87. Quoted in Holzman, *Stormy Ben Butler*, p. 122.

88. Ulysses S. Grant, *Grant*. New York: Literary Classics of the United States, 1990, p. 494.

89. Quoted in Macartney, *Grant and His Generals*, p. 187.

90. Quoted in Holzman, *Stormy Ben Butler*, p. 236.

91. Quoted in Macartney, *Grant and His Generals*, pp. 187–88.

Chapter 5: Unconditional Surrender

92. Williams, *Lincoln and His Generals*, p. 311.

93. William S. McFeely, *Grant*. New York: Norton, 1981, p. 10.

94. Grant, *Grant*, pp. 31–32.

95. Quoted in McFeely, *Grant*, p. 60.

96. Quoted in McFeely, *Grant*, p. 80.

97. Grant, *Grant*, pp. 164–65.

98. Grant, *Grant*, p. 188.

99. Grant, *Grant*, p. 208.

100. Grant, *Grant*, pp. 238–39.

101. Quoted in McFeely, *Grant*, p. 119.

102. Quoted in Burns, *The Civil War*, episode 4.

103. Quoted in Williams, *Lincoln and His Generals*, p. 272.

104. Quoted in McFeely, *Grant*, p. 137.

105. Quoted in McFeely, *Grant*, p. 135.

106. Grant, *Grant*, p. 470.

107. Quoted in Williams, *McClellan, Sherman and Grant*, p. 84.

108. Quoted in Burns, *The Civil War*, episode 6.

109. Quoted in Williams, *McClellan, Sherman and Grant*, p. 107.

110. Quoted in Gabor S. Boritt, ed., *Lincoln's Generals*. New York: Oxford University Press, 1994, p. 168.

111. Quoted in McFeely, *Grant*, p. 165.

112. Quoted in Burns, *The Civil War*, episode 6.

113. Quoted in Williams, *McClellan, Sherman and Grant*, p. 105.

114. Quoted in Burns, *The Civil War*, episode 6.

115. Quoted in Burns, *The Civil War*, episode 6.

116. Quoted in McFeely, *Grant*, p. 217.

117. McFeely, *Grant*, 219.

118. Grant, *Grant*, p. 741.

119. Quoted in McFeely, *Grant*, p. 288.

120. Quoted in McFeely, *Grant*, p. 495.

Chapter 6: Military Genius

121. Quoted in Burke Davis, *Sherman's March*. New York: Random House, 1980, p. 23.

122. William Tecumseh Sherman, *Memoirs of General W. T. Sherman*. New York: Literary Classics of the United States, 1990, p. 16.

123. Quoted in B. H. Liddell Hart, *Sherman; Soldier, Realist, American*. New York: DaCapo Press, 1993, pp. 4–5.

124. Quoted in Hart, *Sherman*, p. 49.

125. Quoted in Hart, *Sherman*, p. 47.

126. Quoted in Hart, *Sherman*, p. 54.

127. Quoted in Hart, *Sherman*, p. 64.

128. Quoted in Davis, *Sherman's March*, p. 15.

129. Quoted in Hart, *Sherman*, p. 74.

130. Quoted in Williams, *McClellan, Sherman and Grant*, p. 59.

131. Quoted in Davis, *Sherman's March*, p. 17

132. Quoted in Hart, *Sherman*, p. 231.

133. Quoted in Hart, *Sherman*, p. 232.

134. Quoted in Williams, *McClellan, Sherman and Grant*, p. 74.

135. Quoted in Hart, *Sherman*, p. 236.

136. Quoted in Davis, *Sherman's March*, p. 31.

137. Quoted in Davis, *Sherman's March*, p. 11.

138. Quoted in Davis, *Sherman's March*, p. 19.

139. Quoted in Davis, *Sherman's March*, p. 18.

140. Quoted in Davis, *Sherman's March*, p. 130.

141. Quoted in Davis, *Sherman's March*, p. 6.

142. Quoted in Davis, *Sherman's March*, p. 25.

143. Quoted in Davis, *Sherman's March*, p. 40.

144. Quoted in Burns, *The Civil War*, episode 7.

145. Quoted in Burns, *The Civil War*, episode 6.

146. Quoted in Burns, *The Civil War*, episode 7.

147. Quoted in Davis, *Sherman's March*, p. 46.

148. Quoted in Davis, *Sherman's March*, p. 45.

149. Quoted in Davis, *Sherman's March*, p. 118.

150. Quoted in Burns, *The Civil War*, episode 7.

151. Quoted in Williams, *McClellan, Sherman and Grant*, p. 75.

152. Quoted in Davis, *Sherman's March*, p. 294.

153. Quoted in Davis, *Sherman's March*, pp. 296–97.

154. Quoted in Davis, *Sherman's March*, p. 298.

155. Quoted in Hart, *Sherman*, p. 422.

156. Quoted in Davis, *Sherman's March*, p. 21.

Chapter 7: Little Phil

157. Quoted in Roy Morris Jr., *Sheridan*. New York: Crown, 1992, p. 1.

158. Quoted in Morris, *Sheridan*, p. 2.

159. Quoted in Morris, *Sheridan*, p. 14.

160. Quoted in Morris, *Sheridan*, p. 22.

161. Quoted in Morris, *Sheridan*, p. 41.

162. Quoted in Morris, *Sheridan*, p. 66.

163. Quoted in Morris, *Sheridan*, pp. 73–74.

164. Quoted in Macartney, *Grant and His Generals*, p. 114.

165. Quoted in Morris, *Sheridan*, p. 174.

166. Quoted in Morris, *Sheridan*, p. 1.

167. Quoted in Morris, *Sheridan*, p. 155.

168. Quoted in Morris, *Sheridan*, p. 156.

169. Quoted in Morris, *Sheridan*, p. 164.

170. Quoted in Morris, *Sheridan*, p. 164.

171. Quoted in Morris, *Sheridan*, pp. 180–81.

172. Quoted in Morris, *Sheridan*, p. 184.

173. Quoted in Morris, *Sheridan*, pp. 201–202.

174. Quoted in Morris, *Sheridan*, p. 229.

175. Quoted in Morris, *Sheridan*, p. 179.

176. Quoted in Morris, *Sheridan*, p. 212.

177. Quoted in Morris, *Sheridan*, p. 213.

178. Quoted in Morris, *Sheridan*, p. 214.

179. Quoted in Macartney, *Grant and His Generals*, p. 119.

180. Quoted in Macartney, *Grant and His Generals*, p. 122.

181. Macartney, *Grant and His Generals*, p. 126.

182. Quoted in Morris, *Sheridan*, p. 256.

183. Quoted in Morris, *Sheridan*, p. 261.

184. Quoted in Morris, *Sheridan*, p. 4.

185. Quoted in Morris, *Sheridan*, p. 393.

186. Quoted in Morris, *Sheridan*, p. 258.

Epilogue: Unsung Heroes

187. Grant, *Grant*, p. 771.

188. Grant, *Grant*, p. 772.

189. Quoted in Willard M. Wallace, *Soul of the Lion*. Gettysburg, PA: Stan Clark Military Books, 1960, p. 202.

FOR FURTHER READING

Timothy Levi Biel, *The Civil War*. San Diego, CA: Lucent, 1991. An overview of the Civil War from its roots to its conclusion at Appomattox Court House. Includes sections on Union generals Grant, Sherman, and others.

Michael Golay, *The Civil War*. New York: Facts On File, 1992. Well-written overview of the Civil War; includes numerous references for further reading.

Albert Marrin, *Unconditional Surrender*. New York: Atheneum, 1994. Biography of Ulysses Grant from his birth to his death due to throat cancer in 1885.

Red Reeder, *The Northern Generals*. New York: Duell, Sloan and Pearce, 1964. Readable account of the Northern leaders of the Civil War from Irvin McDowell to Ulysses Grant.

James P. Reger, *The Battle of Antietam*. San Diego, CA: Lucent, 1997. Account of one of the bloodiest battles of the Civil War; includes material on George McClellan and Ambrose Burnside, both of whom played significant roles in the conflict.

Works Consulted

Gabor S. Boritt, ed., *Lincoln's Generals*. New York: Oxford University Press, 1994. Several distinguished historians contribute essays each dealing with Lincoln and his relationship with a key Union general.

Ken Burns, *The Civil War*. Beverly Hills, CA: Pacific Arts Video, 1990. Compelling and comprehensive film documentary of the Civil War, including quotes and period photos. Available on video in nine episodes. Well worth watching.

Bruce Catton, *This Hallowed Ground*. New York: Doubleday, 1956. Excellent overview of the Civil War from the North's perspective, written by a Pulitzer Prize–winning author.

Burke Davis, *Sherman's March*. New York: Random House, 1980. Complete account of Sherman's march through Georgia and the Carolinas including eyewitness stories from participants on both sides of the conflict.

Ulysses S. Grant, *Grant*. New York: Literary Classics of the United States, 1990. The personal memoirs of U. S. Grant, dealing almost entirely with his life as a soldier, as well as selected letters, many written to his wife, dating from 1839 to 1865. Provides insight into the mind of one of the war's most enigmatic generals.

B. H. Liddell Hart, *Sherman; Soldier, Realist, American*. New York: DaCapo Press, 1993. In-depth study of the character and career of William Tecumseh Sherman from his youth through his death in 1891. Challenging reading.

Robert S. Holzman, *Stormy Ben Butler*. New York: Macmillan, 1954. Objective biography of the controversial general with emphasis on his turbulent civilian and military careers.

Clarence Edward Macartney, *Grant and His Generals*. New York: McBride, 1953. Relationships between general in chief Ulysses S. Grant and the generals he commanded in the last years of the war. Includes chapters on Philip Sheridan, Benjamin Butler, Ambrose Burnside, William Sherman, and others.

William Marvel, *Burnside*. Chapel Hill: University of North Carolina Press, 1991. Biography of the hapless general; the author challenges commonly held views of Burnside as an incompetent leader, seeing him instead as a scapegoat for others' failures.

George B. McClellan, *McClellan's Own Story*. New York: Charles L. Webster, 1887. Revealing autobiography of the general's war years including his views on the conflict, government leaders, and the American people. The work also contains army letters, dispatches, and private correspondence with the author's wife.

William S. McFeely, *Grant*. New York: Norton, 1981. Biography of one of the great heroes of the Civil War, who was a failure in everything but marriage and battle.

Roy Morris Jr., *Sheridan*. New York: Crown, 1992. Full-length biography of the feisty cavalry general who rocketed to fame in the Civil War and later went on to become a controversial leader in operations against Native American tribes in the West.

Dick Nolan, *Benjamin Franklin Butler, the Damnedest Yankee*. Novato, CA: Presidio Press, 1991. Biography of one of the most unpopular generals in the Union army. Emphasizes his unique and important contributions to the war as well as his talents as attorney and administrator before and after the conflict.

Stephen W. Sears, *George B. McClellan, The Young Napoleon*. New York: Ticknor & Fields, 1988. A well-written and complete account of the charismatic but often contradictory general.

William Tecumseh Sherman, *Memoirs of General W. T. Sherman*. New York: Literary Classics of the United States, 1990. Sherman's account of his life through the end of his military career. Includes letters pertaining to the war and firsthand details of the taking of Atlanta and Sherman's march through the South.

Willard M. Wallace, *Soul of the Lion*. Gettysburg, PA: Stan Clark Military Books, 1960. Biography of Joshua Lawrence Chamberlain, respected and beloved scholar/general of the war.

Ezra J. Warner, *Generals in Blue*. Baton Rouge: Louisiana State University Press, 1964. Brief biographies of 583 full-rank generals who served in the Union army during the Civil War. Includes photo or daguerreotype image of each.

T. Harry Williams, *Lincoln and His Generals*. New York: Knopf, 1952. Excellent overview of the Civil War with emphasis on Lincoln's interactions with McClellan, Burnside, Sherman, Grant, and other general officers.

T. Harry Williams, *McClellan, Sherman and Grant*. Rutgers, NJ: Rutgers University Press, 1962. Brief but fascinating look at the careers of three Union generals and how their characters affected their generalship during the Civil War.

PICTURE CREDITS

ABOUT THE AUTHOR

Like many Americans, Diane Yancey finds the Civil War one of the most fascinating and romantic periods of U.S. history. "So many heroes came out of this terrible national upheaval. From the greats like Lincoln, Grant, and Lee to the lesser knowns like Butler and Chamberlain—the people and their stories are endlessly fascinating."

Along with her interest in writing and the Civil War, the author likes to collect old books, travel, and enjoy life in the Pacific Northwest with her husband, two daughters, and two cats. Her other books include *Desperadoes and Dynamite*, *The Hunt for Hidden Killers*, *Life in War-Torn Bosnia*, *Camels for Uncle Sam*, and *Life in a Japanese-American Internment Camp*.